AF446950

Discovering Biblical Treasures

Understanding the Peter Letters

Using Semitic Bible Study Methods with a new foundation

Michael H. Koplitz

Sandra J. Koplitz

This edition 2024 copyright © by Michael H. Koplitz

All rights reserved. No part of this publication may be reproduced or transmitted in any form or by any means without the publisher's permission.

All Scripture quotations, unless otherwise noted, are taken from the *New American Standard Bible®*, Copyright © 1960, 1962, 1963, 1968, 1971, 1972, 1973, 1975, 1977, 1995, 2020 by the Lockman Foundation. Used by permission (www.Lockman.org)

The NASB uses italic to show words that have been added for clarification. Citations are shown with large capital letters.

Published by Michael H. Koplitz

Table of Contents

Introduction

When a person is baptized as an infant and grows up in the church, their religious DNA assimilates different paradigms. The church has a message to give about Jesus Christ and His importance. Very few people study the theology and doctrines of the church to determine for themselves the accuracy of the church. The Proto-Orthodox church, which survived the pressures of the Roman Empire, decided to oppose any expression of Christianity that did not fit its dogma in its infancy. In addition, the Proto-Orthodox church would permanently destroy any writings that the rival Christians had developed.

The Gnostic Christians of Northern Egypt viewed the life of Jesus of Nazareth in a completely different way than the Proto-Orthodox church did. They saw the message about the Kingdom of Heaven as the vital purpose of Jesus. His birth, death, and resurrection are not mentioned in the Gnostic Gospels. However, did the Proto-Orthodox church destroy the Gnostic Gospels when they crushed said movement? The answer is yes and no. Yes, they destroyed what they got their hands on. No, because in 1948, copies of the Gnostic religious books were discovered in Alexandria, Egypt. Once these documents were translated, the world learned what the Gnostic Christians believed. It is fascinatingly different than what the Proto-Orthodox said about these followers of Christ.

Why is this understanding critical? Much research points to a different situation in the early years than what the church espouses. A lot of this information is available to anyone today. However, the Seminaries and churches will not openly discuss these other writings about Jesus and His disciples. The scholars teaching in most Seminaries have learned their lessons from the church and closed-minded mentors who refuse to look at other possibilities. This is because the Western European world took Christianity and changed it from a Near Eastern religion to Western religion.

There is a theory that Paul converted Mithras House Churches into Jesus House Churches. This is clear from the connection between the Mithras' and Christianity's rituals. For example, baptism was the initiation ritual of Mithras. Communion did not originate with Jesus. This ritual was a part of Mithras, where the followers would share his flesh (bread) and drink his blood (wine). There are many more rituals that Christianity picked up from Mithras. A good reference is "Christianity's Need for Mithras," which the author wrote.

Did Paul create the churches in the letters he sent, which comprise the New Testament, and if so, they must have been Jewish groups who became Jewish Christians? They would have continued with their Hebraic rituals and saw Jesus of Nazareth as the Messiah that the prophets of old had promised. They would have adopted many of Jesus' teachings and tried to live by them. The letters in the New Testament are written in Greek. However, most Jews in the Roman Empire did not speak Greek; instead, they spoke Aramaic and Hebrew. These congregations would not have understood a Greek letter from Paul.

Therefore, the letters in the New Testament must have been written in Aramaic and then transliterated into Greek. The same can be said for the Gospels, all of them. The church, over the centuries, decided who wrote the Gospels and their intent. The only Gospel we can assign to a writer is Luke. The other three are up in the air about who wrote them. While in Seminary, the author was taught that the entire New Testament was originally written in Koine Greek. However, that raised the question, "Did Jesus speak Greek?" The Seminary instructors says, "no, Jesus did not speak Greek." Then the New Testament, especially the Gospels, must have been written in Aramaic. After all, Jesus spoke Aramaic and Hebrew.

We know this because He was a poor *tekton* (a stonemason or carpenter) from an impoverished city named Nazareth. Being born to a Jewish family in Galilee, he would have learned the traditions of His people and trade. He would have learned to speak Aramaic, the language of the area. He would have learned Hebrew because that was the language of the synagogue and the Temple in Jerusalem. In other words, Hebrew was the language of God, and Jewish males learned the language.

Suppose you are ready to toss this manuscript into the nearest trash can or delete it off your electronic device at this point in the introduction. In that case, the writer has your attention. This is the reaction when the writer has spoken with persons who had been indoctrinated into the church's position since birth. The author did not come into the church environment until he was 35. Therefore, the church's paradigms, dogma, and doctrine were not a part of his DNA. Instead, he questioned a lot. He found many inconsistencies between the Bible and the doctrines of the church. Seminary was an experience to learn what the church had evolved into two-thousand years after the death of Jesus.

There are more parts to the premise that the New Testament was originally written in Aramaic and will be explored. For the reader to grasp the subsequent phases of the proof, an open mind is critical.

Culture and Language

Let us continue in the journey of examining the New Testament to determine its original language. Nothing in stone tells us that Aramaic is the Original Language of the New Testament. However, nothing says that Koine Greek was the original language of the New Testament either. Therefore, we have two theories about the original language of the New Testament. The author admits that the Seminary he attended drove home the belief that the Old Testament was written in Hebrew, except for a few spots. The New Testament was initially written in Koine Greek.

The writers' research has been searching for the original meaning of Scripture for many years. The methodology for this work is called "Ancient Bible Study Methods." The method was developed by Dr. Anne Davis of the Bible Learning University in Albuquerque, New Mexico. The author studied this method with Dr. Davis as his mentor. It became clear that the search for the original meaning of the Scriptures requires that the culture and language be examined. So, the author's methodology is Dr. Davis' work, plus his Ph.D. studies combining the method, culture, and language.

The language examination is easy for the Old Testament because it was written in Hebrew, and about one-half of Daniel is in Aramaic. It does not take long to realize that idioms and figures of speech in the Hebrew of the Old Testament revealed a lot about the people and situation of the day when the scrolls were written. The Targums were a valuable resource because they are the Aramaic translations the rabbis did for the people living outside of Judea. The rabbis added commentary to the Targums because they knew that some of the idioms and speech used in the Near East would not translate well into the different areas where the Jews lived.

The culture of the Near East has been essentially the same in many aspects since the days of Jesus. Many practices of Jesus' day are still in use today. The culture of the Jews of the Near East is built into the language. Often an Aramaic or Hebrew word has a deep meaning that is only fully understood by natives living in that culture. The Old Testament is filled with cultural items that do not need to be spelled out because the people knew their culture in the author's time.

Suppose the New Testament in Koine Greek is a transliteration of the Aramaic. The culture, figures of speech, and idioms will be easily identified when examining the Peshitta (the Aramaic version of the New Testament). Indeed many of the so-called difficult words of Jesus are not tricky when examined in the light of the culture of Jesus' day. An example is "faith to move a mountain," Jesus says these words to His disciples. The church determined that this meant complete faith in Jesus. From the western European Greek point of view, that makes sense. What else could it possibly mean?

"Faith to move a mountain" is an Aramaic idiomatic expression. What Jesus says to His followers when he says this is that his disciples needed to be faithful so that they could change the "government's view through their words." The governing body for Judaism resided on the top of a mountain. Jerusalem, with its Temple, was built on the top of Mount Zion, a very tall mountain. This idiom survived because the Aramaic Gospels were transliterated into Koine Greek. Numerous other examples support this position.

Suppose the culture and language idioms of Jesus' day can be found in the Koine Greek because it was transliterated. In that case, it supports the theory of the Aramaic versions being the original language of the Gospels and possibly even more.

The Aramaic Version of the New Testament

The Peshitta is the accepted Aramaic translation of the New Testament for many churches of the East. Peshitta means "simple, true, direct, and original." It is a collection of scrolls that were compiled in 150 CE. There were some revisions to the Peshitta in the fifth and sixth centuries. The Greek version of the New Testament is a transliteration of the Peshitta.[1]

For centuries, the Catholic church has used the Latin version of the Bible, the Vulgate, and still uses it. The Vulgate was developed around 350 CE by Jerome by order of the Pope at that time. Erasmus (1466 – 1536) was the person who put together the Greek New Testament for the Catholic church.

"The New Testament, brought to light in the original Greek tongue, was compiled and made available for humanity to study and learn. Although working under and deeply associated with the Roman Catholic Church, the learned scholar declared his disagreement with those who wanted to keep the Scriptures from the common people. He said, "If only the farmer would sing something from them at his plow, the weaver moves his shuttle to their tune, the traveler lighten the boredom of his journey with Scriptural stories!" Little did he know that the work he was about to produce would change the world forever. This Greek New Testament, in printed form, would become the standard of the New Testament, launching the translations of Martin Luther and William Tyndale into the world. Thus, fulfilling his dream that all men would read the

---

[1] Rocco A. Errico and George M. Lamsa, *Aramaic Light on Galatians through Hebrews: A Commentary Based on Aramaic, the Language of Jesus, and Ancient near Eastern Customs* (Smyma, GA: Noohra Foundation, 2005).

Bible for themselves in their common language. His new "study Bible" had two main parts, the Greek text, and a revised Latin edition, which was more elegant and accurate than the traditional translation of Jerome's Latin Vulgate. Erasmus prefaced this monumental work of scholarship with an exhortation to Bible study. He proclaimed that the New Testament contains the "philosophy of Christ," simple and accessible teaching with the power to transform lives."[2]

The church recognized Erasmus' Greek New Testament in 1515 CE. The church in the Near East has been using the Peshitta as the original language of the New Testament since 150 CE. If the Greek New Testament was important to the church as an original language, then why did it adopt the Vulgate in 350 CE? The church should have adopted the Greek New Testament at the beginning.

The Peshitta, translated into English, is used to examine Paul's letters. The rest of the methodology that the author developed for Ancient Bible Study Methods is the framework of this research.

---

[2] "Erasmus Greek New Testament," Insight of the King, accessed February 18, 2022, https://www.insightoftheking.com/erasmus-greek-new-testament.html.

The Messianic Tradition Change

One problem for Peter and the Disciples was that they claimed Yeshua to be the Messiah that the prophets of the Hebrew Scriptures spoke. However, Yeshua did not do what these traditions said. The main tradition was that the Messiah would destroy oppressive Romans and reinstate the Kingdom of Israel. Yeshua would then be declared the king and sit on David's throne in Jerusalem. That did not occur.

None of the messianic traditions of the day worked. So, what was the new movement going to do? They turned to the prophets and discovered Isaiah 50-53. These chapters are referred to as the Suffering Servant chapters. The Yeshua movement decided that the Suffering Servant was Yeshua. The portrayal of Yeshua's life does fit the Suffering Servant chapters. However, rabbinical interpretation then and now sees the Suffering Servant as the nation of Israel. Indeed, these chapters do describe the history of Israel. Nations have wanted to destroy the Jewish people since the time of Abraham.

The diaspora from the Babylonia Exile and the Assyrian invasions looked to squelch the Jewish people. The LORD promised that a remnant of the people would always survive. That is true throughout the 4,000-year history of the Jewish people. Many nations tried to destroy them, and the LORD intervened to ensure that a remnant of the people survived.

Paul must have been convinced in his encounter with Yeshua on the Damascus road that Yeshua was the Suffering Servant. It is clear from Paul's writings that he did believe this. For Paul, the Messiah was the Spiritual Messiah that the Kabbalah spoke. The

Kabbalah says that there will be two Messiahs. This theology is based on Zachariah 9:9. The first Messiah is Messiah ben Joseph. This Messiah was to restore the Kingdom of Heaven, a spiritual Kingdom. The second Messiah will be Messiah ben David. This Messiah was to restore the Kingdom of Israel. The Midrash from the Kabbalah did not state that the Messiah was two different souls.

The Kabbalah

There is a large amount of material in print about the Kabbalah. The Kabbalah referred to is Moses's Secret Work from Mount Sinai. Legends say Moses received three items on Mount Sinai when he met the LORD. The first is the written law. The written law is called the Torah. The second is the oral law. The oral law was put into a written form around 200 CE called the Mishnah. The third is the secret law called the Kabbalah. The secrets of the Kabbalah are based on the Torah and were written down around 200 CE. The main books of the Kabbalah are the Zohar and the Book of Creation.

Many of Yeshua's statements have Kabbalah undertones. Yeshua would have known the Kabbalah. Paul would have known the basics, at least, of the Kabbalah because of his religious education and training.

There are Kabbalistic ideas in the Gospels and Paul's letters. Kabbalistic verses will be highlighted in the chapters of the letters.

Methodology

The methodology employed is to use "Ancient Bible Study Methods" integrated with Jesus's day's customs and culture to examine the Hebrew and Christian Scriptures, thus gathering a more in-depth understanding by learning the Scriptures in the way the people of Jesus's day did.

I have titled the methodology of analyzing a passage of Scripture in a Hebraic manner the "Process of Discovery." The author developed this methodology, which combines various linguistic and cultural understanding areas. There are several sections to the process, and not all the parts apply to every passage of Scripture. The overall result of developing this process is to give the reader a framework for studying the Word in more depth.

The "Process of Discovery" starts with a Scripture passage. An examination of the linguistic structure of the passage is next. The linguistic structure includes parallelism, chiastic structures, and repetition. Formatting the passage in its linguistic form allows the reader to visualize what the first-century CE listener was hearing. Their corresponding sections label the chiasms, for example, A, B, C, B', A.' Not all passages of the Scriptures have a poetic form.

The next step is to "question the narrative." The narrative process of questioning the narrative assumes the reader knows nothing about the passage. Therefore, the questions go from simple to complex. The next task is to identify any linguistic patterns. Linguistic patterns include, but are not limited to, irony, simile, metaphor, symbolism, idioms, hyperbole, figurative language, personification, and allegory.

A review of any translation inconsistencies discovered between the English NAU version and Hebrew or Greek versions is done. Sometimes, a Hebrew or Greek word is translated in more than one way. Inconsistencies also can be created by the translation committee, which may have decided to use traditional language instead of the actual translation. The decision of the translation committee is in the Preface or Introduction to the Bible. Perhaps some of the inconsistencies were intentionally added to convey some deeper meaning. An examination of every discrepancy is done.

The passage is analyzed for any echoes of the Hebrew Scriptures in the Christian Scriptures. An echo occurs using a passage from the Hebrew Scriptures in the Christian Scriptures.[3] Also, echoes are found when Torah (Genesis through Deuteronomy) passages are used in other Hebrew Bible books. Cross-references in the Scripture are references from one verse to another verse, which can help the reader understand the verse.

The names of persons mentioned in the passage are listed. Many Hebrew names have meaning and may be associated with places or actions. Jewish parents used to name their children based on what they felt God had in store for their children. An example is Abraham, whose original name was Abram and was changed to mean eternal father (God changed Abram's name to Abraham, indicating a function he was to perform). When the Hebrew Bible gives names, many occurrences mean something unique. The same importance can occur for the names of places. The time it takes to travel between locations can supply insight into the event.

---

[3] Mitzvot are the 613 commandments found in the Torah that please God. There are positive and negative commandments. The list was first development by Maimonides. The full list can be found at: ttp://www.jewfaq.org/613.htm.

Keyphrases are identified in verses when they are essential to understanding that passage. There are no rules for selecting the keywords. Searching for other occurrences of the keywords in Scripture in concordance is necessary to understand the Word's usage; this must be done in either Hebrew or Greek, not in English. A classic Hebraic approach is to find the usage of a word in the Scripture by finding other verses that contain the Word. The usage of a word in its original language is discovered by searching the Scripture in the language of the Word. Verses that contain the Word are identified, and a pattern for the usage of the Word is discovered. Each verse is examined to see what the usage of the Word is, which may reveal a model for the Word's usage. The first usage of the Word in the Scripture, primarily if used in the Torah, is essential for Hebrew words. The Christian Scriptures are used for Greek words to determine the Word usage in the Scripture. Sometimes, finding the equivalent Greek Word in the Septuagint can be beneficial as analyzing its Hebrew usage.

The Rules of Hillel are used when applicable. Hillel was a Torah scholar who lived shortly before Jesus' day. Hillel developed several rules for Torah students to interpret the Scriptures, which refer to halachic Midrash. In several cases, these rules are helpful in the analysis of the Scripture.

The cultural implications from the writing period are done after the linguistic analysis is completed. The culture is crucial because it is not explicitly referenced in the biblical narratives, as indicated earlier.

From the linguistic analysis and the cultural understanding, it is possible to obtain a deeper meaning of the Scripture beyond the plain text's literal meaning. That is what the listeners of Jesus's time were doing. They put linguistics and culture together without even having to contemplate it.

The analysis will lead to findings explaining the passage's meaning in Jesus's day. Most of the time, the Hebraic analysis leads to the desire for more in-depth analysis to fully understand what Jesus was talking about or what was happening to Him. Whatever the result, a new, more in-depth understanding of the Scripture is obtained.

The components of the Process of Discovery are:

Language

  Process of Discovery

    Linguistics Section

     Linguistic Structure

Discussion

Questioning the Passage

  Verse Comparison of citations or proof text

Translation Inconsistencies

Biblical Personalities

Biblical Locations

Phrase Study

Only the applicable sections are included in this document.

Introduction to the 1 Peter Epistle

The authorship of this letter is in question. If it was written by Peter the apostle, then it must date between 60 and 63 CE. However, various scholars say that this letter could not have been written until at least 70 CE and before 90 CE. Therefore, it is speculation that the apostle Peter wrote this letter. It is a letter that is addressed to the Jewish followers of Yeshua. He emphasizes the death and suffering of Yeshua and the reconciliation that was brought about through the crucifixion and resurrection. Peter referred call Yeshua of the Lamb without a blemish who was foreordained before the foundation of the world. Peter also refers to Yeshua as the cornerstone that was rejected by the builders.

Language

Peshitta	New American Standard 1995
1Pet. 1:1 Peter, a legate of Jesus the Messiah, to the elect and sojourners, who are dispersed in Pontus and in Galatia, and in Cappadocia, and in Asia, and in Bithynia, **2** to them who have been chosen, by the foreknowledge of God the Father, through sanctification of the Spirit, unto the obedience and the sprinkling of the blood of Jesus the Messiah: May grace and peace abound towards you. **3** Blessed be God, the Father of our Lord Jesus the Messiah, who in his great mercy hath begotten us anew, by the resurrection of our Lord Jesus the Messiah, to the hope of life, **4** and to an inheritance incorruptible, undefiled, and unfading, which is prepared for you in heaven; **5** while ye are kept, by the power of God and by faith, for the life that is prepared and will be revealed in the last times; **6** wherein ye will rejoice for ever, notwithstanding ye at the present time are pressed a little, by the various trials that pass over you; **7** so that the proof of your faith may appear more precious than refined gold that is tested by fire, unto glory and honor and praise, at the manifestation of Jesus the Messiah: **8** whom having not seen, ye love; and in the faith of whom ye rejoice, with joy that is glorious and ineffable, **9** that ye may receive the recompense of your faith, the life of your souls; **10** that life [namely], about which the prophets inquired, when they were prophesying of the grace which	**1Pet. 1:1** *a*Peter, an apostle of Jesus Christ, To those who reside as *b*aliens, *c*scattered throughout *d*Pontus, *e*Galatia, *d*Cappadocia, *d*Asia, and *f*Bithynia, *g*who are chosen **2** according to the *a*foreknowledge of God the Father, *b*by the sanctifying work of the Spirit, *1*to *c*obey Jesus Christ and be *d*sprinkled with His blood: *e*May grace and peace *2*be yours in the fullest measure. **1Pet. 1:3** *a*Blessed be the God and Father of our Lord Jesus Christ, who *b*according to His great mercy *c*has caused us to be born again to *d*a living hope through the *e*resurrection of Jesus Christ from the dead, **4** to *obtain* an *a*inheritance *which is* imperishable and undefiled and *b*will not fade away, *c*reserved in heaven for you, **5** who are *a*protected by the power of God *b*through faith for *c*a salvation ready *d*to be revealed in the last time. **6** *a*In this you greatly rejoice, even though now *b*for a little while, *c*if necessary, you have been distressed by *d*various *1*trials, **7** so that the *1a*proof of your faith, *being* more precious than gold which *2*is perishable, *b*even though tested by fire, *c*may be found to result in praise and glory and honor at *d*the revelation of Jesus Christ; **8** and *a*though you have not seen Him, you *b*love Him, and though you do not see Him now, but

was to be given to you. **11** And they searched for the time which the Spirit of the Messiah dwelling in them did show and testify, when the sufferings of the Messiah were to occur, and his subsequent glory. **12** And it was revealed to them, [in regard to] all they were searching, that, not for themselves were they inquiring, but for us they were prophesying of those things, which are now manifested to you by means of the things we have announced to you, by the Holy Spirit sent from heaven; which things the angels also desire to look into. **13** Wherefore, gird up the loins of your minds. and be awake perfectly, and wait for the joy, which will come to you at the revelation of our Lord Jesus the Messiah, **14** as obedient children: and be ye not conversant again with those former lusts, with which ye lusted when without knowledge. **15** But be ye holy in all your conduct, as he is holy who hath called you. **16** Because it is written: Be ye holy, even as I am holy. **17** And if so be ye call on the Father, with whom is no respect of persons, and who judgeth every one according to his deeds, pass the time of your sojournment with fear; **18** since ye know, that neither with perishable silver, nor with gold, ye were redeemed from your vain doings, which ye had by tradition from your fathers; **19** but with the precious blood of that Lamb in which is no spot nor blemish, namely, the Messiah: **20** who was predestined to this, before the foundation of the world; and was manifested at the termination of the times, for your sakes; **21** who, by means of him, have believed in God, who raised him from the dead and conferred glory on him; that your faith and hope might be in God,

believe in Him, you greatly rejoice with joy inexpressible and [1]full of glory, **9** obtaining as [a]the outcome of your faith the salvation of [1]your souls.

1Pet. 1:10 [a]As to this salvation, the prophets who [b]prophesied of the [c]grace that *would come* to you made careful searches and inquiries, **11** [1]seeking to know what person or time [a]the Spirit of Christ within them was indicating as He [b]predicted the sufferings of Christ and the glories [2]to follow. **12** It was revealed to them that they were not serving themselves, but you, in these things which now have been announced to you through those who [a]preached the gospel to you by [b]the Holy Spirit sent from heaven — things into which [c]angels long to [1]look.

1Pet. 1:13 Therefore, [1a]prepare your minds for action, [2b]keep sober *in spirit,* fix your [c]hope completely on the [d]grace [3]to be brought to you at [e]the revelation of Jesus Christ. **14** As [1a]obedient children, do not [2b]be conformed to the former lusts *which were yours* in your [c]ignorance, **15** but [1a]like the Holy One who called you, [2b]be holy yourselves also [c]in all *your* behavior; **16** because it is written, "[a]YOU SHALL BE HOLY, FOR I AM HOLY."

1Pet. 1:17 If you [a]address as Father the One who [b]impartially [c]judges according to each one's work, conduct yourselves [d]in fear during the time of your [e]stay *on earth;* **18** knowing that you were not [1a]redeemed with perishable things like silver or gold from your [b]futile way of life inherited from your forefathers, **19** but with precious [a]blood, as of a [b]lamb unblemished and

[22] while your minds became sanctified, by obedience to the truth; and ye be full of love, without respect of persons, so that ye love one another out of a pure and perfect heart; [23] like persons born again, not of seed that perisheth, but of that which doth not perish, by the living word of God, who abideth for ever. [24] Because all flesh is as grass, and all its beauty like the flower of the field. The grass drieth up, and the flower withereth away; [25] but the word of our God abideth for ever: and this is the word that is announced to you.

spotless, *the blood* of Christ. [20] For He was [a]foreknown before [b]the foundation of the world, but has [c]appeared [1]in these last times [d]for the sake of you [21] who through Him are [a]believers in God, who raised Him from the dead and [b]gave Him glory, so that your faith and [c]hope are in God.

1Pet. 1:22 Since you have [a]in obedience to the truth [b]purified your souls for a [1][c]sincere love of the brethren, fervently love one another from [2]the heart, [23] for you have been [a]born again [b]not of seed which is perishable but imperishable, *that is,* through the living and enduring [c]word of God.

[24]   For,
    "[a]ALL FLESH IS LIKE GRASS,
    AND ALL ITS GLORY LIKE THE FLOWER OF GRASS.
    THE GRASS WITHERS,
    AND THE FLOWER FALLS OFF,
[25]   [a]BUT THE WORD OF THE LORD ENDURES FOREVER."
And this is [b]the word which was [1]preached to you.

1Peter 1:1
[a]2 Pet 1:1
[b]1 Pet 2:11
[c]James 1:1
[d]Acts 2:9
[e]Acts 16:6
[f]Acts 16:7
[g]Matt 24:22; Luke 18:7

1Peter 1:2
[1]Lit *unto obedience and sprinkling*
[2]Lit *be multiplied for you*
[a]Rom 8:29; 1 Pet 1:20
[b]2 Thess 2:13
[c]1 Pet 1:14, 22
[d]Heb 10:22; 12:24
[e]2 Pet 1:2

1Peter 1:3
[a]2 Cor 1:3
[b]Gal 6:16; Titus 3:5
[c]James 1:18; 1 Pet 1:23
[d]1 Pet 1:13, 21; 3:5, 15; 1 John 3:3
[e]1 Cor 15:20; 1 Pet 3:21

1Peter 1:4
[a]Acts 20:32; Rom 8:17; Col 3:24
[b]1 Pet 5:4
[c]2 Tim 4:8

1Peter 1:5
[a]John 10:28; Phil 4:7
[b]Eph 2:8
[c]1 Cor 1:21; 2 Thess 2:13
[d]1 Pet 4:13; 5:1

1Peter 1:6

[1]Or *temptations*
[a]Rom 5:2
[b]1 Pet 5:10
[c]1 Pet 3:17
[d]James 1:2; 1 Pet 4:12

1Peter 1:7
[1]Or *genuineness*
[2]Lit *perishes*
[a]James 1:3
[b]1 Cor 3:13
[c]Rom 2:7
[d]Luke 17:30; 1 Pet 1:13; 4:13

1Peter 1:8
[1]Lit *glorified*
[a]John 20:29
[b]Eph 3:19

1Peter 1:9
[1]One early ms does not contain *your*
[a]Rom 6:22

1Peter 1:10
[a]Matt 13:17; Luke 10:24
[b]Matt 26:24
[c]1 Pet 1:13

1Peter 1:11
[1]Or *inquiring*
[2]Lit *after these*
[a]2 Pet 1:21
[b]Matt 26:24

1Peter 1:12
[1]Or *gain a clear glimpse*
[a]1 Pet 1:25; 4:6
[b]Acts 2:2-4
[c]1 Tim 3:16

1Peter 1:13

[1]Lit *gird the loins of your mind*
[2]Lit *be sober*
[3]Or *which is announced*
[a]Eph 6:14
[b]1 Thess 5:6, 8; 2 Tim 4:5; 1 Pet 4:7; 5:8
[c]1 Pet 1:3
[d]1 Pet 1:10
[e]1 Pet 1:7

1Peter 1:14
[1]Lit *children of obedience*
[2]Or *conform yourselves*
[a]1 Pet 1:2
[b]Rom 12:2; 1 Pet 4:2f
[c]Eph 4:18

1Peter 1:15
[1]Lit *according to*
[2]Or *become*
[a]1 Thess 4:7; 1 John 3:3
[b]2 Cor 7:1
[c]James 3:13

1Peter 1:16
[a]Lev 11:44f; 19:2; 20:7

1Peter 1:17
[a]Ps 89:26; Jer 3:19; Matt 6:9
[b]Acts 10:34
[c]Matt 16:27
[d]2 Cor 7:1; Heb 12:28; 1 Pet 3:15
[e]1 Pet 2:11

1Peter 1:18
[1]Or *ransomed*
[a]Is 52:3; 1 Cor 6:20; Titus 2:14; Heb 9:12
[b]Eph 4:17

1Peter 1:19
[a]Acts 20:28; 1 Pet 1:2
[b]John 1:29

1Peter 1:20
[1]Lit *at the end of the times*
[a]Acts 2:23; Eph 1:4; 1 Pet 1:2; Rev 13:8
[b]Matt 25:34
[c]Heb 9:26
[d]Heb 2:14

1Peter 1:21
[a]Rom 4:24; 10:9
[b]John 17:5, 24; 1 Tim 3:16; Heb 2:9
[c]1 Pet 1:3

1Peter 1:22
[1]Lit *unhypocritical*
[2]Two early mss read *a clean heart*
[a]1 Pet 1:2
[b]James 4:8
[c]John 13:34; Rom 12:10; Heb 13:1; 1 Pet 2:17; 3:8

1Peter 1:23
[a]John 3:3; 1 Pet 1:3
[b]John 1:13
[c]Heb 4:12

1Peter 1:24
[a]Is 40:6ff; James 1:10f

1Peter 1:25
[1]Lit *preached as good news to you*
[a]Is 40:8
[b]Heb 6:5

1Pet. 1:0 ΠΕΤΡΟΥ ΕΠΙΣΤΟΛΗ ΠΡΩΤΗ

1Pet. 1:1   Πετρος αποστολος Ιησου Χριστου εκλεκτοις παρεπιδημοις διασπορας Ποντου, Γαλατιας, Καππαδοκιας, Ασιας και Βιθυνιας [2] κατα προγνωσιν θεου πατρος εν αγιασμω πνευματος εις υπακοην και ραντισμον αιματος Ιησου Χριστου, χαρις υμιν και ειρηνη πληθυνθειη.

1Pet. 1:3   Ευλογητος ο θεος και πατηρ του κυριου ημων Ιησου Χριστου ο κατα το πολυ αυτου ελεος αναγεννησας ημας εις ελπιδα ζωσαν δι' αναστασεως Ιησου Χριστου εκ νεκρων [4] εις κληρονομιαν αφθαρτον και αμιαντον και αμαραντον τετηρημενην εν ουρανοις εις υμας [5] τους εν δυναμει θεου φρουρουμενους δια πιστεως εις σωτηριαν ετοιμην αποκαλυφθηναι εν καιρω εσχατω [6] εν ω αγαλλιασθε, ολιγον αρτι, ει δεον εστιν, λυπηθεντας εν ποικιλοις πειρασμοις, [7] ινα το δοκιμιον υμων της πιστεως πολυτιμοτερον χρυσιου του απολλυμενου, δια πυρος δε δοκιμαζομενου ευρεθη εις επαινον και δοξαν και τιμην εν αποκαλυψει Ιησου Χριστου [8] ον ουκ ιδοντες αγαπατε, εις ον αρτι μη ορωντες, πιστευοντες δε αγαλλιασθε χαρα ανεκλαλητω και δεδοξασμενη [9] κομιζομενοι το τελος της πιστεως υμων σωτηριαν ψυχων. [10] περι ης σωτηριας εξεζητησαν και εξηραυνησαν προφηται οι περι της εις υμας χαριτος προφητευσαντες [11] εραυνωντες εις τινα η ποιον καιρον εδηλου το εν αυτοις πνευμα Χριστου προμαρτυρομενον τα εις Χριστον παθηματα και τας μετα ταυτα δοξας. [12] οις απεκαλυφθη οτι ουχ εαυτοις, υμιν δε διηκονουν αυτα α νυν ανηγγελη υμιν δια των ευαγγελισαμενων υμας εν πνευματι αγιω αποσταλεντι απ' ουρανου, εις α επιθυμουσιν αγγελοι παρακυψαι.

1Pet. 1:13   Διο αναζωσαμενοι τας οσφυας της διανοιας υμων νηφοντες τελειως ελπισατε επι την φερομενην υμιν χαριν εν αποκαλυψει Ιησου Χριστου. [14] ως τεκνα υπακοης μη συσχηματιζομενοι ταις προτερον εν τη αγνοια υμων επιθυμιαις, [15] αλλα κατα τον καλεσαντα υμας αγιον και αυτοι αγιοι εν παση αναστροφη γενηθητε, [16] διοτι γεγραπται· *αγιοι εσεσθε, οτι εγω αγιος.* [17] και ει πατερα επικαλεισθε τον απροσωπολημπτως κρινοντα κατα το εκαστου εργον, εν φοβω τον της παροικιας υμων χρονον αναστραφητε

1Pet. 1:18   ειδοτες οτι ου φθαρτοις, αργυριω η χρυσιω, ελυτρωθητε
εκ της ματαιας υμων αναστροφης πατροπαραδοτου
[19] αλλα τιμιω αιματι ως αμνου αμωμου και ασπιλου Χριστου
[20] προεγνωσμενου μεν προ καταβολης κοσμου,
φανερωθεντος δε επ' εσχατου των χρονων
δι' υμας [21] τους δι' αυτου πιστους εις θεον

τον εγειραντα αυτον εκ νεκρων και δοξαν αυτω δοντα,
ωστε την πιστιν υμων και ελπιδα ειναι εις θεον.

1Pet. 1:22   Τας ψυχας υμων ηγνικοτες εν τη υπακοη της αληθειας εις φιλαδελφιαν ανυποκριτον εκ καθαρας καρδιας αλληλους αγαπησατε εκτενως [23] αναγεγεννημενοι ουκ εκ σπορας φθαρτης αλλ' αφθαρτου δια λογου ζωντος θεου και μενοντος. [24] διοτι

 πασα σαρξ ως χορτος
  και πασα δοξα αυτης ως ανθος χορτου·
 εξηρανθη ο χορτος και το ανθος εξεπεσεν·
[25] *το δε ρημα κυριου μενει εις τον αιωνα.*

τουτο δε εστιν το ρημα το ευαγγελισθεν εις υμας.

Language

  Process of Discovery

    Linguistics Section

      Linguistic Structure

1Pet. 1:1   *ª*Peter, an apostle of Jesus Christ,

A To those who reside as *ᵇ*aliens, *ᶜ*scattered throughout *ᵈ*Pontus, *ᵉ*Galatia, *ᵈ*Cappadocia, *ᵈ*Asia, and *ᶠ*Bithynia, *ᵍ*who are chosen ² according to the *ª*foreknowledge of God the Father, *ᵇ*by the sanctifying work of the Spirit, ¹to *ᶜ*obey Jesus Christ and be *ᵈ*sprinkled with His blood: *ᵉ*May grace and peace ²be yours in the fullest measure.

> **B**³ Blessed be the God and Father of our Lord Jesus Christ, who *ᵇ*according to His great mercy *ᶜ*has caused us to be born again to *ᵈ*a living hope through the *ᵉ*resurrection of Jesus Christ from the dead, ⁴ to *obtain* an *ª*inheritance *which is* imperishable and undefiled and *ᵇ*will not fade away, *ᶜ*reserved in heaven for you,

A⁵ who are *ª*protected by the power of God *ᵇ*through faith for *ᶜ*a salvation ready *ᵈ*to be revealed in the last time.

> **B** ⁶ *ª*In this you greatly rejoice, even though now *ᵇ*for a little while, *ᶜ*if necessary, you have been distressed by *ᵈ*various ¹trials,

>> **C**⁷ so that the ¹*ª*proof of your faith, *being* more precious than gold which ²is perishable, *ᵇ*even though tested by fire, *ᶜ*may be found to result in praise and glory and honor at *ᵈ*the revelation of Jesus Christ;

> **B'**⁸ and *ª*though you have not seen Him, you *ᵇ*love Him, and though you do not see Him now, but believe in Him, you greatly rejoice with joy inexpressible and ¹full of glory,

A'⁹ obtaining as *ª*the outcome of your faith the salvation of ¹your souls.

A ¹⁰ *ª*As to this salvation, the prophets

> **B** who *ᵇ*prophesied of the *ᶜ*grace that *would come* to you made careful searches and inquiries,

C [11] [1]seeking to know what person or time [a]the Spirit of Christ within them was indicating as He [b]predicted the sufferings of Christ and the glories [2]to follow.

B' [12] It was revealed to them that they were not serving themselves, but you, in these things which now have been announced to you through those who [a]preached the gospel to you by [b]the Holy Spirit sent from heaven —

A' things into which [c]angels long to [1]look.

A [13] Therefore, [1a]prepare your minds for action, [2b]keep sober *in spirit,* fix your [c]hope completely on the [d]grace [3]to be brought to you at [e]the revelation of Jesus Christ.

B [14] As [1a]obedient children, do not [2b]be conformed to the former lusts *which were yours* in your [c]ignorance,

C [15] but [1a]like the Holy One who called you, [2b]be holy yourselves also [c]in all *your* behavior; [16] because it is written, "[a]YOU SHALL BE HOLY, FOR I AM HOLY."

B' [17] If you [a]address as Father the One who [b]impartially [c]judges according to each one's work, conduct yourselves [d]in fear during the time of your [e]stay *on earth;*

A' [18] knowing that you were not [1a]redeemed with perishable things like silver or gold from your [b]futile way of life inherited from your forefathers, [19] but with precious [a]blood, as of a [b]lamb unblemished and spotless, *the blood* of Christ.

A [20] For He was [a]foreknown before [b]the foundation of the world, but has [c]appeared [1]in these last times [d]for the sake of you [21] who through Him are [a]believers in God, who raised Him from the dead and [b]gave Him glory, so that your faith and [c]hope are in God.

B [22] Since you have [a]in obedience to the truth [b]purified your souls for a [1c]sincere love of the brethren, fervently love one another from [2]the heart, [23] for you have been [a]born again [b]not of seed which is perishable but imperishable, *that is,* through the living and enduring [c]word of God.

A' [24]   For,
"[a]ALL FLESH IS LIKE GRASS,
AND ALL ITS GLORY LIKE THE FLOWER OF GRASS.
THE GRASS WITHERS,
AND THE FLOWER FALLS OFF,

²⁵ "BUT THE WORD OF THE LORD ENDURES FOREVER."
And this is ^bthe word which was ¹preached to you.

Discussion

This chapter has several chiasms in it. It is a wordy chapter.

Questioning the Passage

1. Who are the dispersed people? (v. 1)

    The Assyrian invasion of the northern kingdom of Israel and the invasion by Babylon into the southern kingdom of Israel caused the people to be scattered throughout the known world. Today, these people are known as the diaspora, but in the author's time, they were called dispersed people. Therefore, these are Jews who were living outside of Judea or Galilee.

2. Who was the letter addressed to? (v. 1)

    Scholars believe that the author of this letter targeted Jews living in Asia Minor. From the New Testament's point of view, the only people who were evangelized were those from the Near East through the Roman Empire.

3. Why was the letter not sent to Babylonia, Greece or Rome? (v. 1)

    Evangelists that Yeshua sent out only went into Syria and Asia minor (when Yeshua sent the 70 persons out). This letter showed it was addressed to mainly Asia minor communities.

4. Who was the audience for this letter? (v. 1)

The audiences of this letter are Jews who were evangelized into believing that Yeshua was the Messiah that the Hebrew Scriptures call for.

5. What is the definition of the "chosen" in verse two?

The word chosen used in this verse is synonymous with the word the elect from the Christian tradition. The idea of election according to ancestry and tribal dissent the author emphasizes that the acceptance of the gospel is what will give a person truly election. Jews who had accepted the gospel of Yeshua became heirs of the promise that God made to Abraham and to David.

A part of church tradition is that one had to be accepted into the elite by God before one was born. There are several theological positions about when the selection happened. One belief is that all souls that would ever exist on the earth were created before the earth was created. God knew which of the souls would become part of the elect. A second theology says that souls are created as history plays out. God then selects the elect from the souls that are born each day.

In the time of Martin Luther, there was a very interesting debate between Luther and the Pope about who was guaranteed entrance into heaven. However, excommunication by the church was a way to change a person's election status. Luther and the Pope excommunicated each other from the church.

6. What is the definition of sanctifying? (v. 2)

Sanctification means being made right before God. Once a person accepts Yeshua as Lord and Savior, a baptism ritual is performed. This gives justifying grace to the individual. It is believed that the Holy Spirit then comes upon the person, like it did upon Yeshua in the Gospels, and leads the soul forward to becoming perfect. Only souls that are perfect may be in heaven because God is perfect. Therefore, sanctifying grace is quite important to have.

7. What does "to obey Jesus Christ and be sprinkled with His blood? Mean" (v. 2)

This is a metaphor for the cleansing of sins through the sacrifice of Yeshua.

8. What does it mean to be bound in grace and peace? (v. 3)

This refers to God's abundant mercy, which is the basis for the blessings that follow. Therefore, God's abundant mercy is shown by the blessings that shower down from heaven.

9. What does "hope of life" mean (a living hope [NRSV])? (v. 3)

Yeshua has caused us to be born again to a living hope: This speaks to the concept of being "born again" or regenerated through faith in Christ. The "living hope" refers to the eternal life and inheritance believers have through Christ.

10. What does verse five mean?

"Who through faith" refers to believers who have put their faith in Christ's finished work. It's their faith that saved them when they first trusted in Him as Savior.

"Are shielded by God's power" speaks to the protection provided by God's power. Believers are defended as if in a fortress or castle. This protection is not passive but active, implying that God is actively working to guard believers.

"Until the coming of the salvation" refers to the ultimate salvation or deliverance that believers will experience. This salvation is not just from the penalty of sin, but also from the power of sin in their lives.

"That is ready to be revealed in the last time" suggests that the fullness of this salvation is yet to be revealed and will be fully known in the "last time", often interpreted as the end times or the return of Christ.

This verse, therefore, speaks to the protective power of God for those who have faith, guarding them until the ultimate salvation is revealed.[4]

11. What are the various trails? (v. 6)

Changing one's religion in Yeshua's day was a big deal. It was rarely done because when it happened, the nuclear family would toss that person out. Therefore, the Jews in Asia minor who came to call Yeshua the Messiah would have to endure family difficulties. They would be persecuted by the local synagogue for their faith, and there was the possibility of death.

12. What does verse seven mean?

The proof for one's faith in Yeshua was day was that one stayed with the faith no matter what the persecutions were.

---

[4] 1. "1 Peter 1:5 - Verse-by-Verse Bible Commentary," StudyLight.org, accessed July 5, 2024, https://www.studylight.org/commentary/1-peter/1-5.html.

13. What does "joy that is glorious" ("full of glory") mean? (v. 8)

The author was saying to the people that if they stayed with Yeshua, even though there were those trials and persecutions that they would be full of glory, meaning that they would receive sanctification and forgiveness of sins through their faith.

14. What does verse ten mean in the Peshitta vs. NASB and NRSV?

Christian tradition says that when the prophets spoke about the coming of the Messiah, that they equated it to receiving the grace of God through forgiveness of sins.

15. What does verse eleven mean?

The prophets were trying to understand who or when the "Spirit of Christ in them" was indicating. They scrutinized their own writings to find the content and timing of the coming of the Messiah.

The Spirit of Christ in them refers to the Holy Spirit, also known as the Spirit of Christ, who was working in the prophets, guiding them in their prophecies.

The Spirit of Christ in the prophets was predicting the sufferings that Christ would endure and the glories that would follow. These predictions were about the death and resurrection of Jesus Christ, and the salvation that would come through Him.

This verse, therefore, speaks to the prophetic anticipation of the sufferings and glories of Christ. It underscores the mystery and the divine revelation involved in the message of salvation.[5]

16. What does verse twelve mean?

The author believed that the angels in heaven wanted to see the glorious things that were revealed by Yeshua's gospel through the faithful men who are preaching it. This would show that God's mystery of salvation through Yeshua was hidden even from the angels.[6]

17. What does "gird up the loins of your minds" mean? (v. 13)

The author writes in metaphorical language because he is a Near Eastern author. In his day, men wore breastplates to protect themselves. When men went into battle, they wore breastplates to protect themselves. The author encourages Yeshua's followers to wear the armor of the Holy Spirit which was considered stronger than any weapon of war and to be constantly on the alert for persecutions. They were to fill their minds with the truth that Yeshua taught so they could understand the message.[7]

18. What is the revelation of Yeshua? (v. 13)

The revelation of Yeshua was the understanding of the salvation that was offered through his death and resurrection.

---

[5] 1. "1 Peter 1:11," BibleRef.com, accessed July 5, 2024, https://www.bibleref.com/1-Peter/1/1-Peter-1-11.html.
[6] 1. Aramaic light on james through revelation: Rocco A. Errico and George M. Lamsa: 9780976008026: Amazon.com: Books, accessed July 5, 2024, https://www.amazon.com/Aramaic-Light-James-through-Revelation/dp/0976008025.
[7] IBID.

19. What were the former lusts? (v. 14)

The author is advising the readers to let go of materialistic items that they felt they had to have. There is a difference between needs and wants. The author is referring to the wants in this case. Many of the ancient ways were in violation of God's basic law, the Torah. Therefore, as followers of Yeshua, they needed to rid themselves of those sins.

20. How does verse fifteen differ from God's foreknowledge?

This verse is referring to God's foreknowledge that Yeshua needed to be sent to save the world from its sins.

21. What does verse eighteen and nineteen mean?

This verse is used for substitute theology. Gold or silver, which is precious even today, could not be used to buy back our souls from all the sins that we have done. Only God sacrificing himself on a cross could do it.

22. What does verse twenty and twenty-one mean?

Jesus Christ, who was known and loved by God before the creation of the world. The term "foreknown" here means that God had complete knowledge ahead of time of who Christ is and what He would do on earth. Jesus Christ, in God's timing, came to earth for the benefit of those who would believe in Him. The "last times" refers to the period starting with Christ's first coming to earth at His birth and ending with Christ's Second Coming to earth to establish His Kingdom.

Jesus Christ is not only the object of their faith but also the means or agency of their belief in God. These believers would have professed belief in God prior to believing in Jesus. It would seem now that their belief in Jesus has allowed them to see God as He is and believe in Him in a new way that is real and true.

The work of Jesus Christ—His death, resurrection, and glorification—leads to faith and hope in God. These verses, therefore, speak to the foreknowledge of God, the manifestation of Jesus Christ, the role of believers, and the resurrection and glorification of Jesus Christ.[8]

23. What does "born again" mean in verse twenty-three?

This is an idiom which means to be regenerated to become like little children having to relearn everything they thought they knew. Therefore, to be born again means to have an incorruptible faith in God. In the northern Galilee, there is an Aramaic idiom that means to change one's thoughts and habits.

Verse Comparison of citations or proof text

1. **5** but [1a]like the Holy One who called you, [2b]be holy yourselves also [c]in all *your* behavior; **16** because it is written, "[a]YOU SHALL BE HOLY, FOR I AM HOLY."

   Leviticus 11:44 'For [a]I am the LORD your God. Consecrate yourselves therefore, and [b]be holy, for I am holy. And you shall not make yourselves unclean with any of the swarming things that swarm on the earth.

[8] 1. The Bible Says, "1 Peter 1:20-21 Meaning," TheBibleSays.com, June 13, 2024, https://thebiblesays.com/en/commentary/1pe+1:20?slug=null.

2. **24**   For, FLOWER OF GRASS. THE GRASS WITHERS, AND THE FLOWER FALLS OFF,**25**   [a]BUT THE WORD OF THE LORD ENDURES FOREVER." And this is [b]the word which was [1]preached to you.

Isaiah 40:66   A voice says, "Call out." Then [1]he answers, "What shall I call out?" [a]All flesh is grass, and all its [2]loveliness is like the flower of the field

Thoughts

This chapter deals with several topics. It opens with the understanding of salvation and hope in the resurrection of Yeshua. It then discusses the trials that the faithful will have to go through because they came to know Yeshua as their Savior. Towards the end of the chapter, it discusses how the prophets viewed the coming Messiah and the call to holiness. If you are going through trials in your life, looking at Yeshua to help you get through them would be in line with the thoughts of this chapter.

Language

Peshitta	New American Standard 1995
1Pet. 2:1 Therefore, cease ye from all malice, and all guile, and hypocrisy, and envy, and backbiting. **2** And be like infant children; and crave the word, as being the pure spiritual milk by which ye are nourished up to life; **3** if ye have tasted and seen that the Lord is good: **4** to whom ye have come, because he is a living stone, rejected indeed by men, but with God elect and precious. **5** And ye also, as living stones, are builded and become spiritual temples, and holy priests, for the offering of spiritual sacrifices, acceptable before God, through Jesus the Messiah. **6** For it is said in the scripture, Behold, in Zion I lay a chosen and precious stone, for the head of the corner; and whoever believeth in him, will not be ashamed. **7** On you therefore who believe, is this honor conferred: but to them who believe not, **8** he is a stone of stumbling and a rock of offence. And they stumble at it, because they believe not the word: whereto they were appointed. **9** But ye are an elect race, officiating as priests of the kingdom; a holy people, a redeemed congregation; that ye should proclaim the praises of him who called you out of darkness to his precious light: **10** who formerly were not accounted a people, but now are the people of God; and also, there were [once] no mercies on you, but now mercies are poured out upon you. **11** My beloved, I	**1Pet. 2:1** Therefore, [a]putting aside all [1]malice and all deceit and [2]hypocrisy and [2]envy and all [2b]slander, **2** [a]like newborn babies, long for the [1b]pure [2]milk of the word, so that by it you may [c]grow [3]in respect to salvation, **3** if you have [a]tasted [1b]the kindness of the Lord. **1Pet. 2:4** And coming to Him as to a living stone which has been [a]rejected by men, but is [1]choice and precious in the sight of God, **5** [a]you also, as living stones, [1]are being built up as a [b]spiritual house for a holy [c]priesthood, to [d]offer up spiritual sacrifices acceptable to God through Jesus Christ. **6** For *this* is contained in [1]Scripture: "[a]BEHOLD, I LAY IN ZION A CHOICE STONE, A [b]PRECIOUS CORNER *stone,* AND HE WHO BELIEVES IN [2]HIM WILL NOT BE [3]DISAPPOINTED." **7** [a]This precious value, then, is for you who believe; but for those who disbelieve, "[b]THE STONE WHICH THE BUILDERS [c]REJECTED, THIS BECAME THE VERY CORNER *stone,*" **8** and, "[a]A STONE OF STUMBLING AND A ROCK OF OFFENSE";

entreat you as strangers and pilgrims, separate yourselves from all lusts of the body; for they war against the soul. **12** And let your behavior be decorous before all men; so that they who utter evil speeches against you, may see your good actions, and may praise God in the day of trial. **13** And be ye submissive to all the sons of men, for God's sake; to kings, on account of their authority; **14** and to judges, because they are sent by him for the punishment of offenders, and for the praise of them that do well. **15** For so is the pleasure of God, that by your good deeds ye may stop the mouth of the foolish, who know not God: **16** as free men, yet not like men who make their freedom a cloak for their wickedness, but as the servants of God. **17** Honor all men; love your brethren; fear God; and honor kings. **18** And those among you who are servants, be subject to your masters, with reverence; not only to the good and gentle, but also to the harsh and morose. **19** For there is favor before God for them who, for the sake of a good conscience, endure sorrows that come upon them wrongfully. **20** But they who endure afflictions on account of their offences, what praise have they? But if, when ye do well, they vex you, and ye endure it; then great is your praise with God. **21** For unto this were ye called; because the Messiah also died for us, and left us this pattern, that ye should walk in his steps. **22** He did no sin; neither was guile found in his mouth. **23** When he was reviled, be reviled not; and he suffered and threatened not, but committed his cause to the Judge of righteousness. **24** And he took away all our sins, and, in his body, lifted them to the cross; that we, when dead to sin, might live

*b*for they stumble because they are disobedient to the word, *c*and to this *doom* they were also appointed.

1Pet. 2:9 But you are *a*A CHOSEN RACE, A royal *b*PRIESTHOOD, A *c*HOLY NATION, *d*A PEOPLE FOR *God's* OWN POSSESSION, so that you may proclaim the excellencies of Him who has called you *e*out of darkness into His marvelous light; **10** *a*for you once were NOT A PEOPLE, but now you are THE PEOPLE OF GOD; you had NOT RECEIVED MERCY, but now you have RECEIVED MERCY.

1Pet. 2:11 *a*Beloved, *b*I urge you as *c*aliens and strangers to abstain from *d*fleshly lusts which wage *e*war against the soul. **12** *a*Keep your behavior excellent among the Gentiles, so that in the thing in which they *b*slander you as evildoers, they may *1*because of your good deeds, as they observe *them,* *c*glorify God *d*in the day of *2*visitation.

1Pet. 2:13 *a*Submit yourselves for the Lord's sake to every human institution, whether to a king as the one in authority, **14** or to governors as sent *1*by him *a*for the punishment of evildoers and the *b*praise of those who do right. **15** For *1a*such is the will of God that by doing right you may *b*silence the ignorance of foolish men. **16** *Act* as *a*free men, and *1*do not use your freedom as a covering for evil, but *use it* as *b*bondslaves of God. **17** *a*Honor all people, *b*love the brotherhood, *c*fear God, *d*honor the *1*king.

by his righteousness: for by his wounds, ye are healed. **25** For ye, [once] went astray, like sheep; but ye have now returned to the Shepherd and Curator of your souls.

1Pet. 2:18 [a]Servants, be submissive to your masters with all respect, not only to those who are good and [b]gentle, but also to those who are [1]unreasonable. **19** For this *finds* [1]favor, if for the sake of [a]conscience toward God a person bears up under sorrows when suffering unjustly. **20** For what credit is there if, when you sin and are harshly treated, you endure it with patience? But if [a]when you do what is right and suffer *for it* you patiently endure it, this *finds* [1]favor with God. **21** For [a]you have been called for this purpose, [b]since Christ also suffered for you, leaving you [c]an example for you to follow in His steps, **22** WHO [a]COMMITTED NO SIN, NOR WAS ANY DECEIT FOUND IN HIS MOUTH; **23** [1]and while being [a]reviled, He did not revile in return; while suffering, He uttered no threats, but kept entrusting *Himself* to Him who judges righteously; **24** and He Himself [1][a]bore our sins in His body on the [2][b]cross, so that we [c]might die to [3]sin and live to righteousness; for [d]by His [4]wounds you were [e]healed. **25** For you were [a]continually straying like sheep, but now you have returned to the [b]Shepherd and [1]Guardian of your souls.

1Peter 2:1
[1]Or *wickedness*
[2]plural nouns
[a]Eph 4:22, 25, 31; James 1:21
[b]James 4:11

1Peter 2:2
[1]Or *unadulterated*
[2]Or *spiritual* (Gr *logikos*) *milk*
[3]Or *up to salvation*
[a]Matt 18:3; 19:14; Mark 10:15; Luke 18:17; 1 Cor 14:20
[b]1 Cor 3:2
[c]Eph 4:15f

1Peter 2:3
[1]Lit *that the Lord is kind*
[a]Heb 6:5
[b]Ps 34:8; Titus 3:4

1Peter 2:4
[1]Lit *chosen;* or *elect*
[a]1 Pet 2:7

1Peter 2:5
[1]Or *allow yourselves to be built up;* or *build yourselves up*
[a]1 Cor 3:9
[b]Gal 6:10; 1 Tim 3:15
[c]Is 61:6; 66:21; 1 Pet 2:9; Rev 1:6
[d]Rom 15:16; Heb 13:15

1Peter 2:6
[1]Or *a scripture*
[2]Or *it*
[3]Or *put to shame*
[a]Is 28:16; Rom 9:32, 33; 10:11; 1 Pet 2:8
[b]Eph 2:20

1Peter 2:7

*a*2 Cor 2:16; 1 Pet 2:7, 8
*b*Ps 118:22; Matt 21:42; Luke 2:34
*c*1 Pet 2:4

1Peter 2:8
*a*Is 8:14
*b*1 Cor 1:23; Gal 5:11
*c*Rom 9:22

1Peter 2:9
*a*Is 43:20f; Deut 10:15
*b*Is 61:6; 66:21; 1 Pet 2:5; Rev 1:6
*c*Ex 19:6; Deut 7:6
*d*Ex 19:5; Deut 4:20; 14:2; Titus 2:14
*e*Is 9:2; 42:16; Acts 26:18; 2 Cor 4:6

1Peter 2:10
*a*Hos 1:10; 2:23; Rom 9:25; 10:19

1Peter 2:11
*a*Heb 6:9; 1 Pet 4:12
*b*Rom 12:1
*c*Lev 25:23; Ps 39:12; Eph 2:19; Heb 11:13; 1 Pet 1:17
*d*Rom 13:14; Gal 5:16, 24
*e*James 4:1

1Peter 2:12
[1]Or *as a result of*
[2]I.e. Christ's coming again in judgment
*a*2 Cor 8:21; Phil 2:15; Titus 2:8; 1 Pet 2:15; 3:16
*b*Acts 28:22
*c*Matt 5:16; 9:8; John 13:31; 1 Pet 4:11, 16
*d*Is 10:3; Luke 19:44

1Peter 2:13
*a*Rom 13:1

1Peter 2:14
[1]Lit *through*
*a*Rom 13:4
*b*Rom 13:3

1Peter 2:15
[1]Lit *so*
[a]1 Pet 3:17
[b]1 Pet 2:12

1Peter 2:16
[1]Lit *not having*
[a]John 8:32; James 1:25
[b]Rom 6:22; 1 Cor 7:22

1Peter 2:17
[1]Or *emperor*
[a]Rom 12:10; 13:7
[b]1 Pet 1:22
[c]Prov 24:21
[d]Matt 22:21; 1 Pet 2:13

1Peter 2:18
[1]Or *perverse*
[a]Eph 6:5
[b]James 3:17

1Peter 2:19
[1]Or *grace*
[a]Rom 13:5; 1 Pet 3:14, 16f

1Peter 2:20
[1]V 19, note 1
[a]1 Pet 3:17

1Peter 2:21
[a]Acts 14:22; 1 Pet 3:9
[b]1 Pet 3:18; 4:1, 13
[c]Matt 11:29; 16:24

1Peter 2:22
[a]Is 53:9; 2 Cor 5:21

1Peter 2:23
[1]Lit *who*

*Is 53:7; Heb 12:3; 1 Pet 3:9

1Peter 2:24
[1]Or *carried...up to the cross*
[2]Lit *wood*
[3]Lit *sins*
[4]Lit *wound;* or *welt*
*Is 53:4, 11; 1 Cor 15:3; Heb 9:28
[b]Acts 5:30
*Rom 6:2, 13
[d]Is 53:5
*Heb 12:13; James 5:16

1Peter 2:25
[1]Or *Bishop, Overseer*
*Is 53:6
[b]John 10:11; 1 Pet 5:4

Koine Greek

1Pet. 2:1   Αποθεμενοι ουν πασαν κακιαν και παντα δολον και υποκρισεις και φθονους και πασας καταλαλιας [2] ως αρτιγεννητα βρεφη το λογικον αδολον γαλα επιποθησατε, ινα εν αυτω αυξηθητε εις σωτηριαν, [3] *ει εγευσασθε οτι χρηστος ο κυριος.* [4] προς ον προσερχομενοι λιθον ζωντα υπο ανθρωπων μεν αποδεδοκιμασμενον, παρα δε θεω εκλεκτον εντιμον, [5] και αυτοι ως λιθοι ζωντες οικοδομεισθε οικος πνευματικος εις ιερατευμα αγιον ανενεγκαι πνευματικας θυσιας ευπροσδεκτους θεω δια Ιησου Χριστου. [6] διοτι περιεχει εν γραφη·

ιδου τιθημι εν Σιων λιθον ακρογωνιαιον εκλεκτον εντιμον,

και ο πιστευων επ' αυτω ου μη καταισχυνθη.

[7] υμιν ουν η τιμη τοις πιστευουσιν, απιστουσιν δε *λιθος ον απεδοκιμασαν οι οικοδομουντες, ουτος εγενηθη εις κεφαλην γωνιας* [8] και *λιθος προσκομματος και πετρα σκανδαλου·* οι προσκοπτουσιν τω λογω απειθουντες εις ο και ετεθησαν. [9] υμεις δε γενος εκλεκτον, βασιλειον ιερατευμα, εθνος αγιον, λαος εις *περιποιησιν, οπως τας αρετας* εξαγγειλητε του εκ σκοτους υμας καλεσαντος εις το θαυμαστον αυτου φως· [10] οι ποτε *ου λαος, νυν δε λαος θεου, οι ουκ ηλεημενοι, νυν δε ελεηθεντες.*

1Pet. 2:11   Αγαπητοι, παρακαλω ως παροικους και παρεπιδημους απεχεσθαι των σαρκικων επιθυμιων αιτινες στρατευονται κατα της ψυχης· [12] την αναστροφην υμων εν τοις εθνεσιν εχοντες καλην, ινα εν ω καταλαλουσιν υμων ως κακοποιων εκ των καλων εργων εποπτευοντες δοξασωσιν τον θεον *εν ημερα επισκοπης.*

1Pet. 2:13   Υποταγητε παση ανθρωπινη κτισει δια τον κυριον, ειτε βασιλει ως υπερεχοντι [14] ειτε ηγεμοσιν ως δι' αυτου πεμπομενοις εις εκδικησιν κακοποιων, επαινον δε αγαθοποιων, [15] οτι ουτως εστιν το θελημα του θεου αγαθοποιουντας φιμουν την των αφρονων ανθρωπων αγνωσιαν, [16] ως ελευθεροι και μη ως επικαλυμμα εχοντες της κακιας την ελευθεριαν αλλ' ως θεου δουλοι. [17] παντας τιμησατε, την αδελφοτητα αγαπατε, τον θεον φοβεισθε, τον βασιλεα τιματε.

1Pet. 2:18   Οι οικεται υποτασσομενοι εν παντι φοβω τοις δεσποταις, ου μονον τοις αγαθοις και επιεικεσιν αλλα και τοις σκολιοις. [19] τουτο γαρ χαρις, ει δια συνειδησιν θεου υποφερει τις λυπας πασχων αδικως. [20] ποιον γαρ κλεος, ει αμαρτανοντες και κολαφιζομενοι υπομενειτε; αλλ' ει αγαθοποιουντες και πασχοντες υπομενειτε, τουτο χαρις παρα θεω. [21]

εις τουτο γαρ εκληθητε,

οτι και Χριστος επαθεν υπερ υμων

υμιν υπολιμπανων υπογραμμον,

ινα επακολουθησητε τοις ιχνεσιν αυτου,

[22] ος αμαρτιαν *ουκ εποιησεν*

ουδε ευρεθη δολος εν τω στοματι αυτου,
23 *ος λοιδορουμενος ουκ αντελοιδορει,*
πασχων ουκ ηπειλει,
παρεδιδου δε τω κρινοντι δικαιως,
24 *ος τας αμαρτιας ημων αυτος ανηνεγκεν*
εν τω σωματι αυτου επι το ξυλον,
ινα ταις αμαρτιαις απογενομενοι
τη δικαιοσυνη ζησωμεν,
ου τω μωλωπι ιαθητε.
25 *ητε γαρ ως προβατα πλανωμενοι,*
αλλ᾽ επεστραφητε νυν επι τον ποιμενα
και επισκοπον των ψυχων υμων.

Language

Process of Discovery

Linguistics Section

Linguistic Structure

[Exhortation] [1] Therefore, *a*putting aside all [1]malice and all deceit and [2]hypocrisy and [2]envy and all [2b]slander, [2] *a*like newborn babies, long for the [1b]pure [2]milk of the word, so that by it you may *c*grow [3]in respect to salvation, [3] if you have *a*tasted [1b]the kindness of the Lord.

[Citation] [4] And coming to Him as to a living stone which has been *a*rejected by men, but is [1]choice and precious in the sight of God, [5] *a*you also, as living stones, [1]are being built up as a *b*spiritual house for a holy *c*priesthood, to *d*offer up spiritual sacrifices acceptable to God through Jesus Christ.

[6]   For *this* is contained in [1]Scripture:

"*a*BEHOLD, I LAY IN ZION A CHOICE STONE, A *b*PRECIOUS CORNER *stone*,

AND HE WHO BELIEVES IN [2]HIM WILL NOT BE [3]DISAPPOINTED."

[7] *a*This precious value, then, is for you who believe; but for those who disbelieve,

"*b*THE STONE WHICH THE BUILDERS *c*REJECTED,

THIS BECAME THE VERY CORNER *stone*,"

[8]   and,

"*a*A STONE OF STUMBLING AND A ROCK OF OFFENSE";

*b*for they stumble because they are disobedient to the word, *c*and to this *doom* they were also appointed. [9] But you are *a*A CHOSEN RACE, A royal *b*PRIESTHOOD, A *c*HOLY NATION, *d*A PEOPLE FOR *God's* OWN POSSESSION, so that you may proclaim the excellencies of Him who has called you *e*out of darkness into His marvelous light; [10] *a*for you once were NOT A PEOPLE, but now you are THE PEOPLE OF GOD; you had NOT RECEIVED MERCY, but now you have RECEIVED MERCY.

[Exhortation] [11] *a*Beloved, *b*I urge you as *c*aliens and strangers to abstain from *d*fleshly lusts which wage *e*war against the soul. [12] *a*Keep your behavior excellent among the Gentiles, so that in the thing in which they *b*slander you as evildoers, they may [1]because of your good deeds, as they observe *them*, *c*glorify God *d*in the day of [2]visitation.

[Submit to the governmane] [13] *a*Submit yourselves for the Lord's sake to every human institution, whether to a king as the one in authority, [14] or to governors as sent [1]by him *a*for the punishment of evildoers and the *b*praise of those who do right. [15] For [1a]such is the will of God that by doing right you may *b*silence the ignorance of foolish men. [16] *Act* as *a*free men, and [1]do not use your freedom as a covering for evil, but *use it* as

^bbondslaves of God. **17** ^aHonor all people, ^blove the brotherhood, ^cfear God, ^dhonor the ¹king.

[Servants] **18** ^aServants, be submissive to your masters with all respect, not only to those who are good and ^bgentle, but also to those who are ¹unreasonable. **19** For this *finds* ¹favor, if for the sake of ^aconscience toward God a person bears up under sorrows when suffering unjustly. **20** For what credit is there if, when you sin and are harshly treated, you endure it with patience? But if ^awhen you do what is right and suffer *for it* you patiently endure it, this *finds* ¹favor with God. **21** For ^ayou have been called for this purpose, ^bsince Christ also suffered for you, leaving you ^can example for you to follow in His steps, **22** WHO ^aCOMMITTED NO SIN, NOR WAS ANY DECEIT FOUND IN HIS MOUTH; **23** ¹and while being ^areviled, He did not revile in return; while suffering, He uttered no threats, but kept entrusting *Himself* to Him who judges righteously; **24** and He Himself ^{1a}bore our sins in His body on the ^{2b}cross, so that we ^cmight die to ³sin and live to righteousness; for ^dby His ⁴wounds you were ^ehealed. **25** For you were ^acontinually straying like sheep, but now you have returned to the ^bShepherd and ¹Guardian of your souls.

Discussion

This chapter is a continuation of the exhortations found in the first chapter.

Questioning the Passage

1. What is "spiritual milk?" (v. 2)

    Spiritual milk refers to the basic, foundational truths of God's Word that nourish our souls. Just as infants crave and thrive on their mother's milk, baby Christians should crave and delight in the simple truths of Scripture. This spiritual milk is pure and unadulterated, providing the essential nutrients for spiritual growth. It encompasses teachings related to righteousness through Jesus and other fundamental principles of God. These include:

    - Righteousness by Faith Through Jesus Christ

    - Repentance from Dead Works

- Faith Toward God

- Doctrine of Baptisms

- Laying On of Hands

- The Resurrection of the Dead

- Eternal Judgment

Spiritual milk as the ABCs of the Bible—the foundational knowledge that helps believers grow and mature in their faith. Understanding righteousness correctly is crucial, as it sets the perspective for comprehending the rest of the spiritual milk teachings.

2. What is the kindness of the Lord? (v. 3)

This phrase is an invitation from the Lord to savor spiritual nourishment which is found with Him. It is a reminder to appreciate God's kindness and experience His presence in our live.

3. What is a living stone? (v. 4)

This idiom means a "strong stone." Strong stones were difficult to hew. Builders rejected these stones for the foundation of buildings.

4. What does verse five mean?

Peter uses a powerful metaphor to describe believers. He refers to them as "living stones" being built into a spiritual house.

Just as Jesus is the "living stone," Christians are also living. We were once spiritually dead but have been made alive through God's grace and faith in Christ. Our physical death is not the end; our resurrection is assured by God's promise.

God is currently constructing a spiritual dwelling place for Himself, made up of His people. This new temple is not a physical building but a community of believers. We are part of this spiritual house.

In the Old Testament, priests represented the people before God. Now, all barriers have been removed. As believers, we serve as priests, offering spiritual sacrifices directly to God through Jesus. We come to God "in Jesus' name," presenting our offerings on His authority. Our righteousness comes from Him.

5. What does verse twelve mean?

The apostle Peter encourages believers to maintain honorable conduct among non-believers. By living uprightly and demonstrating good deeds, even when slandered, Christians can ultimately bring glory to God. The idea is that our behavior matters, and the world is watching how we live our lives . So, it's a call to be a positive example, even in challenging circumstances.[9]

6. What does verse sixteen mean?

The apostle Peter emphasizes that Christian freedom should not be used as a license for wrongdoing. Instead, believers should willingly obey constituted authorities, recognizing that true liberty comes from God . So, it's a call to live as free people while remaining respectful and obedient to the governing authorities.

7. How do we deal with verse eighteen today?

Peter addresses Christian servants (or slaves) and instructs them to be subject to their masters with all respect. This submission applies not only to kind and considerate masters but also to those who are harsh or unjust. Essentially, it's a

---

9 1. "1 Peter 2:12," BibleRef.com, accessed July 17, 2024, https://www.bibleref.com/1-Peter/2/1-Peter-2-12.html.

call for willing subjection, rooted in reverence for God, rather than fear of man. The culture of Peter's day allowed for slavery in many different expressions. Slavery as an open practice does not exist today. There are types of slavery that do exist in the darkness which means the government is unaware of it or cannot stop it.

However, a person can feel like a slave at the workplace. When this happens, it is time to search for an alternative employer.

8. How does Yeshua's suffering apply to people who are not slaves or not being beaten? (v. 20 – 21)

At the time of the writing of this epistle becoming a followers of Yeshua had a heavy cost. History says that many of the original followers left the order because of the persecution from their family or the Roman government. The author is connecting the followers suffering with the ultimate suffering Yeshua experienced. Therefore, a follower of Yeshua should expect suffering to test their faith.

9. Could verses twenty-four and twenty-five be a redaction since the letter was written to Jews since Yeshua's death for the forgiveness of sin was from Mithras? Jewish communities had the animal sacrifice system until 70 CE when the Romans destroyed the Temple at Jerusalem. It is historical fact that Jewish-Christians brought sacrifices for sin to Jerusalem. It was not a belief that the Messiah would die for the forgiveness of sin. This concept entered Christianity when Paul's converted Mithras churches became the majority of influence in the emerging Proto-Orthodox church.

Therefore, the community the author was writing to comes into question. Another view is that these verses were redacted to the original letter when the Proto-Orthodox church decided to include it in the newly forming Scriptural cannon.

The Jewish part of the community would have believed in the Tashlich. This was a promise from the LORD that His chosen people would always be forgive for their sin. These verses are clearly for the Mithra converts.

Verse Comparison of citations or proof text

1. [6] For *this* is contained in [1]Scripture: "[a]BEHOLD, I LAY IN ZION A CHOICE STONE, A [b]PRECIOUS CORNER *stone,* AND HE WHO BELIEVES IN [2]HIM WILL NOT BE [3]DISAPPOINTED."

   Isaiah 28:16 Therefore thus says the Lord [1]GOD, "[a]Behold, I am laying in Zion a stone, a tested [b]stone, a costly cornerstone for the foundation, [2]firmly placed. He who believes in it will not be [3]disturbed.

2. [7] [a]This precious value, then, is for you who believe; but for those who disbelieve, "[b]THE STONE WHICH THE BUILDERS [c]REJECTED, THIS BECAME THE VERY CORNER *stone,*"

   Psa. 118:22 The [a]stone which the builders rejected has become the chief corner stone.

3. [8] and, "[a]A STONE OF STUMBLING AND A ROCK OF OFFENSE"; [b]for they stumble because they are disobedient to the word, [c]and to this *doom* they were also appointed.

   Isaiah 8:14 "Then He shall become a [a]sanctuary; But to both the houses of Israel, a [b]stone to strike and a rock to stumble over, And a snare and a [c]trap for the inhabitants of Jerusalem.

4. ^{9} But you are ^{a}A CHOSEN RACE, A royal ^{b}PRIESTHOOD, A ^{c}HOLY NATION, ^{d}A PEOPLE FOR *God's* OWN POSSESSION, so that you may proclaim the excellencies of Him who has called you ^{e}out of darkness into His marvelous light;

Deut 10:15"Then He shall become a ^{a}sanctuary; But to both the houses of Israel, a ^{b}stone to strike and a rock to stumble over, and a snare and a ^{c}trap for the inhabitants of Jerusalem.

5. ^{10} ^{a}for you once were NOT A PEOPLE, but now you are THE PEOPLE OF GOD; you had NOT RECEIVED MERCY, but now you have RECEIVED MERCY.

Hosea 2:23 "And I will ^{a}sow her for Myself in the land. ^{b}I will also have compassion on ^{1}her who had not obtained compassion, and ^{c}I will say to ^{2}those who were ^{d}not My people, 'You are My people!' and ^{3}they will say, 'Thou art my God!'"

6. ^{22} WHO ^{a}COMMITTED NO SIN, NOR WAS ANY DECEIT FOUND IN HIS MOUTH;

Isaiah 59:3 For your ^{a}hands are defiled with blood, And your fingers with iniquity; your lips have spoken ^{b}falsehood, your tongue mutters wickedness.

Thoughts

This chapter contains a list of exhortations which are an attempt to get the Roman government to accept Christianity in the same manner as it accepted Judaism.

Language

Peshitta	New American Standard 1995
1Pet. 3:1 So also ye wives, be ye subject to your husbands; that, by your pleasing behavior, ye may gain over, without difficulty, those who obey not the word, **2** when they see, that ye conduct yourselves with reverence and chastity. **3** And adorn not yourselves with the external ornaments of curls of the hair, or of golden trinkets, or of costly garments. **4** But adorn yourselves in the hidden person of the heart, with a mild and uncorrupted spirit, an ornament that is precious before God. **5** For so also the holy women of old, who trusted in God, adorned themselves, and were subject to their husbands: **6** just as Sarah was subject to Abraham, and called him, My lord: whose daughters ye are, by good works, while ye are not terrified by any fear. **7** And ye husbands, likewise, dwell with your wives according to knowledge, and hold them in honor, as the feebler vessels; because they also will inherit with you the gift of eternal life: and let not your prayers be hindered. **8** The summing up, is, that ye all be in harmony, that ye be sympathetic with them who suffer, and affectionate one to another, and be merciful and kind. **9** And that ye recompense to no one evil for evil, neither railing for railing; but, in contrariety to these, that ye bless: for to this were ye called, that ye might inherit a blessing. **10** Therefore, whoever chooseth life, and desireth to see good days, let him keep his	**1Pet. 3:1** *a*In the same way, you wives, *b*be submissive to your own husbands so that even if any *of them* are disobedient to the word, they may be *c*won without a word by the behavior of their wives, **2** as they observe your chaste and [1]respectful behavior. **3** *a*Your adornment must not be *merely* external — braiding the hair, and wearing gold jewelry, or putting on dresses; **4** but *let it be a*the hidden person of the heart, with the imperishable quality of a gentle and quiet spirit, which is precious in the sight of God. **5** For in this way in former times the holy women also, *a*who hoped in God, used to adorn themselves, being submissive to their own husbands; **6** just as Sarah obeyed Abraham, *a*calling him lord, and you have become her children if you do what is right [1]*b*without being frightened by any fear. **1Pet. 3:7** *a*You husbands in the same way, live with *your wives* in an understanding way, as with [1]*b*someone weaker, since she is a woman; and show her honor as a fellow heir of the grace of life, so that your prayers will not be hindered. **1Pet. 3:8** [1]To sum up, *a*all of you be harmonious, sympathetic, *b*brotherly, *c*kindhearted, and *d*humble in spirit; **9** *a*not returning evil for evil or *b*insult for insult, but [1]giving a *c*blessing instead; for *d*you

tongue from evil, and his lips that they speak no guile; **11** let him turn away from evil, and do good; let him seek peace, and follow after it. **12** Because the eyes of the Lord are upon the righteous, and his ears [ready] to hear them: but the face of the Lord is against the wicked. **13** And who will do you harm, if ye are zealous of good works? **14** But if it should occur, that ye suffer on account of righteousness, happy are ye. And be not terrified, by those who would terrify you, nor be agitated: **15** but sanctify the Lord the Messiah, in your hearts. And be ye ready for a vindication, before every one who demandeth of you an account of the hope of your faith, **16** in meekness and respect, as having a good conscience; so that they who speak against you as bad men, may be ashamed, for having calumniated your good conduct in the Messiah. **17** For it is profitable to you, that ye suffer evil while ye do good deeds, if this should be the pleasure of God; and not, while ye do evil deeds. **18** For the Messiah also once died for our sins, the righteous for sinners; that he might bring you to God. And he died in body, but lived in spirit. **19** And he preached to those souls, which were detained in Hades, **20** which were formerly disobedient, in the days of Noah, when the long suffering of God commanded an ark to be made, in hope of their repentance; and eight souls only entered into it, and were kept alive in the waters. **21** And ye also, by a like figure, are made alive by baptism, (not when ye wash your bodies from filth, but when ye confess God with a pure conscience,) and by the resurrection of Jesus the Messiah; **22** who is taken up to heaven, and is on the

were called for the very purpose that you might ^cinherit a blessing.

10   For,

"^aTHE ONE WHO DESIRES LIFE, TO LOVE AND SEE GOOD DAYS,

MUST KEEP HIS TONGUE FROM EVIL AND HIS LIPS FROM SPEAKING DECEIT.

11   "^aHE MUST TURN AWAY FROM EVIL AND DO GOOD;

HE MUST SEEK PEACE AND PURSUE IT.

12   "^aFOR THE EYES OF THE LORD ARE TOWARD THE RIGHTEOUS,

AND HIS EARS ATTEND TO THEIR PRAYER,

BUT THE FACE OF THE LORD IS AGAINST THOSE WHO DO EVIL."

1Pet. 3:13 ^aWho is ¹there to harm you if you prove zealous for what is good? **14** But even if you should ^asuffer for the sake of righteousness, ^byou ¹are blessed. ^cAND DO NOT FEAR THEIR ²INTIMIDATION, AND DO NOT BE TROUBLED, **15** but ¹sanctify ^aChrist as Lord in your hearts, always *being* ready ^bto make a ²defense to everyone who asks you to give an account for the ^chope that is in you, yet ^cwith gentleness and ^{3d}reverence; **16** ¹and keep a ^agood conscience so that in the thing in which ^byou are slandered, those who revile your good behavior in Christ will be put to shame. **17** For ^ait is better, ^bif ¹God should will it so, that you suffer for doing what is right rather than for doing what is wrong. **18** For ^aChrist also died for sins ^bonce for all, *the* just for *the* unjust, so

right hand of God, and angels, and authorities, and powers, are subject to him.	that He might *b*bring us to God, having been put to death *d*in the flesh, but made alive *e*in the [1]spirit; **19** in [1]which also He went and made proclamation to the spirits *now* in prison, **20** who once were disobedient, when the *a*patience of God *b*kept waiting in the days of Noah, during the construction of *c*the ark, in which a few, that is, *d*eight *e*persons, were brought safely through *the* [1]water. **21** *a*Corresponding to that, baptism now saves you — *b*not the removal of dirt from the flesh, but an appeal to God [1]for a *c*good conscience — through *d*the resurrection of Jesus Christ, **22** *a*who is at the right hand of God, *b*having gone into heaven, *c*after angels and authorities and powers had been subjected to Him.

1Peter 3:1
[a]1 Pet 3:7
[b]Eph 5:22; Col 3:18
[c]1 Cor 9:19

1Peter 3:2
[1]Lit *with respect*

1Peter 3:3
[a]Is 3:18ff; 1 Tim 2:9

1Peter 3:4
[a]Rom 7:22

1Peter 3:5
[a]1 Tim 5:5; 1 Pet 1:3

1Peter 3:6
[1]Lit *and are not*
[a]Gen 18:12
[b]1 Pet 3:14

1Peter 3:7
[1]Lit *a weaker vessel*
[a]Eph 5:25; Col 3:19
[b]1 Thess 4:4

1Peter 3:8
[1]Or *Finally*
[a]Rom 12:16
[b]1 Pet 1:22
[c]Eph 4:32
[d]Eph 4:2; Phil 2:3; 1 Pet 5:5

1Peter 3:9
[1]Lit *blessing instead*
[a]Rom 12:17; 1 Thess 5:15
[b]1 Cor 4:12; 1 Pet 2:23

[c]Luke 6:28; Rom 12:14; 1 Cor 4:12
[d]1 Pet 2:21
[e]Gal 3:14; Heb 6:14; 12:17

1Peter 3:10
[a]Ps 34:12, 13

1Peter 3:11
[a]Ps 34:14

1Peter 3:12
[a]Ps 34:15, 16

1Peter 3:13
[1]Lit *the one who will harm you*
[a]Prov 16:7

1Peter 3:14
[1]Or *would be*
[2]Lit *fear*
[a]Matt 5:10; 1 Pet 2:19ff; 4:15f
[b]James 5:11
[c]Is 8:12f; 1 Pet 3:6

1Peter 3:15
[1]I.e. set apart
[2]Or *argument;* or *explanation*
[3]Or *fear*
[a]1 Pet 1:3
[b]Col 4:6
[c]2 Tim 2:25
[d]1 Pet 1:17

1Peter 3:16
[1]Lit *having a good*
[a]1 Tim 1:5; Heb 13:18; 1 Pet 3:21
[b]1 Pet 2:12, 15

1Peter 3:17
[1]Lit *the will of God*
[a]1 Pet 2:20; 4:15f

^bActs 18:21; 1 Pet 1:6; 2:15; 4:19

1Peter 3:18
[1]Or *Spirit*
^a1 Pet 2:21
^bHeb 9:26, 28; 10:10
^cRom 5:2; Eph 3:12
^dCol 1:22; 1 Pet 4:1
^e1 Pet 4:6

1Peter 3:19
[1]Or *whom*

1Peter 3:20
[1]I.e. the great flood
^aRom 2:4
^bGen 6:3, 5, 13f
^cHeb 11:7
^dGen 8:18; 2 Pet 2:5
^eActs 2:41; 1 Pet 1:9, 22; 2:25; 4:19

1Peter 3:21
[1]Or *from*
^aActs 16:33; Titus 3:5
^bHeb 9:14; 10:22
^c1 Tim 1:5; Heb 13:18; 1 Pet 3:16
^d1 Pet 1:3

1Peter 3:22
^aMark 16:19
^bHeb 4:14; 6:20
^cRom 8:38f; Heb 1:6

Koine Greek

1Pet. 3:1   Ομοιως αι γυναικες, υποτασσομεναι τοις ιδιοις ανδρασιν, ινα και ει τινες απειθουσιν τω λογω, δια της των γυναικων αναστροφης ανευ λογου κερδηθησονται [2] εποπτευσαντες την εν φοβω αγνην αναστροφην υμων. [3] ων εστω ουχ ο εξωθεν εμπλοκης τριχων και περιθεσεως χρυσιων η ενδυσεως ιματιων κοσμος, [4] αλλ' ο κρυπτος της καρδιας ανθρωπος εν τω αφθαρτω του πραεως και ησυχιου πνευματος ο εστιν ενωπιον του θεου πολυτελες. [5] ουτως γαρ ποτε και αι αγιαι γυναικες αι ελπιζουσαι εις θεον εκοσμουν εαυτας υποτασσομεναι τοις ιδιοις ανδρασιν, [6] ως Σαρρα υπηκουσεν τω Αβρααμ κυριον αυτον καλουσα ης εγενηθητε τεκνα αγαθοποιουσαι και μη φοβουμεναι μηδεμιαν πτοησιν.

1Pet. 3:7   Οι ανδρες ομοιως, συνοικουντες κατα γνωσιν ως ασθενεστερω σκευει τω γυναικειω, απονεμοντες τιμην ως και συγκληρονομοις χαριτος ζωης εις το μη εγκοπτεσθαι τας προσευχας υμων.

1Pet. 3:8   Το δε τελος παντες ομοφρονες, συμπαθεις, φιλαδελφοι, ευσπλαγχνοι, ταπεινοφρονες, [9] μη αποδιδοντες κακον αντι κακου η λοιδοριαν αντι λοιδοριας, τουναντιον δε ευλογουντες, οτι εις τουτο εκληθητε, ινα ευλογιαν κληρονομησητε.

[10]   ο γαρ θελων ζωην αγαπαν
       και ιδειν ημερας αγαθας
   παυσατω την γλωσσαν απο κακου
       και χειλη του μη λαλησαι δολον,
[11]   εκκλινατω δε απο κακου και ποιησατω αγαθον,
       ζητησατω ειρηνην και διωξατω αυτην·
[12]   οτι οφθαλμοι κυριου επι δικαιους
       και ωτα αυτου εις δεησιν αυτων,
   προσωπον δε κυριου επι ποιουντας κακα.

1Pet. 3:13   Και τις ο κακωσων υμας, εαν του αγαθου ζηλωται γενησθε; [14] αλλ' ει και πασχοιτε δια δικαιοσυνην, μακαριοι. *τον δε φοβον αυτων μη φοβηθητε μηδε ταραχθητε,* [15] *κυριον δε τον Χριστον αγιασατε* εν ταις καρδιαις υμων, ετοιμοι αει προς απολογιαν παντι τω αιτουντι υμας λογον περι της εν υμιν ελπιδος, [16] αλλα μετα πραυτητος και φοβου, συνειδησιν εχοντες αγαθην, ινα εν ω καταλαλεισθε καταισχυνθωσιν οι επηρεαζοντες υμων την αγαθην εν Χριστω αναστροφην. [17] κρειττον γαρ αγαθοποιουντας, ει θελοι το θελημα του θεου, πασχειν η κακοποιουντας.

[18]   οτι και Χριστος απαξ περι αμαρτιων επαθεν,
       δικαιος υπερ αδικων,
   ινα υμας προσαγαγη τω θεω
       θανατωθεις μεν σαρκι,
   ζωοποιηθεις δε πνευματι·
[19]   εν ω και τοις εν φυλακη πνευμασιν

πορευθεις εκηρυξεν
[20] απειθησασιν ποτε, οτε απεξεδεχετο η του θεου μακροθυμια εν ημεραις Νωε κατασκευαζομενης κιβωτου εις ην ολιγοι, τουτ' εστιν οκτω ψυχαι, διεσωθησαν δι' υδατος [21] ο και υμας αντιτυπον νυν σωζει βαπτισμα, ου σαρκος αποθεσις ρυπου αλλα συνειδησεως αγαθης επερωτημα εις θεον, δι' αναστασεως Ιησου Χριστου [22] ος εστιν εν δεξια του θεου πορευθεις εις ουρανον υποταγεντων αυτω αγγελων και εξουσιων και δυναμεων.

Language

  Process of Discovery

    Linguistics Section

    Linguistic Structure

[Exhortation to women] [1a]In the same way, you wives, [b]be submissive to your own husbands so that even if any *of them* are disobedient to the word, they may be [c]won without a word by the behavior of their wives, **2** as they observe your chaste and [1]respectful behavior. **3** [a]Your adornment must not be *merely* external — braiding the hair, and wearing gold jewelry, or putting on dresses; **4** but *let it be* [a]the hidden person of the heart, with the imperishable quality of a gentle and quiet spirit, which is precious in the sight of God. **5** For in this way in former times the holy women also, [a]who hoped in God, used to adorn themselves, being submissive to their own husbands; **6** just as Sarah obeyed Abraham, [a]calling him lord, and you have become her children if you do what is right [1b]without being frightened by any fear.

[Husband exhortation] **7** [a]You husbands in the same way, live with *your wives* in an understanding way, as with [1b]someone weaker, since she is a woman; and show her honor as a fellow heir of the grace of life, so that your prayers will not be hindered.

[Summary] 1Pet. 3:8 [1]To sum up, [a]all of you be harmonious, sympathetic, [b]brotherly, [c]kindhearted, and [d]humble in spirit; **9** [a]not returning evil for evil or [b]insult for insult, but [1]giving a [c]blessing instead; for [d]you were called for the very purpose that you might [e]inherit a blessing.

10   For,
        "[a]THE ONE WHO DESIRES LIFE, TO LOVE AND SEE GOOD DAYS,
         MUST KEEP HIS TONGUE FROM EVIL AND HIS LIPS FROM
SPEAKING DECEIT.
11   "[a]HE MUST TURN AWAY FROM EVIL AND DO GOOD;
         HE MUST SEEK PEACE AND PURSUE IT.
12   "[a]FOR THE EYES OF THE LORD ARE TOWARD THE RIGHTEOUS,
         AND HIS EARS ATTEND TO THEIR PRAYER,
         BUT THE FACE OF THE LORD IS AGAINST THOSE WHO DO EVIL."

1Pet. 3:13 [a]Who is [1]there to harm you if you prove zealous for what is good? **14** But even if you should [a]suffer for the sake of righteousness, [b]you [1]are blessed. [c]AND DO NOT FEAR THEIR [2]INTIMIDATION, AND DO NOT BE TROUBLED, **15** but [1]sanctify [a]Christ as Lord in your hearts, always *being* ready [b]to make a [2]defense to everyone who asks you to give an account for the [a]hope that is in you, yet [c]with gentleness and [3d]reverence; [16] [1]and keep a [a]good conscience so that in the thing in which [b]you are slandered, those who revile your good behavior in Christ will be put to shame. [17] For [a]it is better, [b]if [1]God should will it so, that you suffer for doing what is right rather than for doing what is wrong. [18] For [a]Christ also died for sins [b]once for all, *the* just for *the* unjust, so that He might [c]bring us to God, having been put to death [d]in the flesh, but made alive [e]in the [1]spirit; [19] in [1]which also He went and made proclamation to the spirits *now* in prison, [20] who once were disobedient, when the [a]patience of God [b]kept waiting in the days of Noah, during the construction of [c]the ark, in which a few, that is, [d]eight [e]persons, were brought safely through *the* [1]water. [21] [a]Corresponding to that, baptism now saves you — [b]not the removal of dirt from the flesh, but an appeal to God [1]for a [c]good conscience — through [d]the resurrection of Jesus Christ, [22] [a]who is at the right hand of God, [b]having gone into heaven, [c]after angels and authorities and powers had been subjected to Him.

Discussion

This chapter is a continuation of exhortations from the author.

Questioning the Passage

1. What does it mean to be submissive to your husband? (v. 1)

    This verse encourages wives to be submissive to their husbands, hoping their respectful and godly behavior might influence their husbands, even if the husbands are not believers. Actions can sometimes speak louder than words, and a wife's conduct can be a powerful testimony of her faith. This verse was not intended to demand that wives follow their husbands blindly. It is saying that wives should not dismiss their husbands' needs in the name of Christ. Rather, show the love of Christ in the relationship.

2. How does the wife respond to a husband who insists she does something against her beliefs? (v. 1)

This is a challenging situation, and it's important to approach it with wisdom and grace. Here are some steps a Christian wife might consider.

a. Seek God's wisdom and strength through prayer. Request clarity and the right words to communicate your beliefs to your husband.

b. Express your concerns and beliefs to your husband in a respectful and loving manner when you feel uncomfortable with his request and how it conflicts with your faith.

c. Consult with a trusted pastor, church leader, or Christian counselor. They can provide guidance and support, helping you navigate difficult situations.

d. It's important to set healthy boundaries. If your husband insists on something that opposes your core beliefs, kindly but firmly stand your ground.

e. Continue to show Christ-like love and behavior. Your actions can be a powerful testimony of your faith and may influence your husband positively.

f. If the situation involves any form of abuse or coercion, prioritize your safety. Seek help from trusted friends, family, or authorities if necessary.

3. What does it mean "to adorn yourself" in verse five?

This refers to women who wanted to show off their wealth.

4. What fear does not make one afraid? (v. 6)

The author is referring to Sarah from the book of Genesis in that she always did good and was not afraid of any intimidation or fear because she was following God. Christian women should do the same. Following Yeshua was difficult in the early years of Christianity because so many people were against it. Intimidation should not stop a person from worshiping Yeshua.

5. What does verse seven mean?

Husbands are encouraged to live with their wives in an understanding manner. This involves recognizing and valuing their wives' feelings, needs, and perspectives. The term "weaker vessel" refers to physical strength, as women were considered physically weaker than men. However, this does not imply inferiority. Instead, it emphasizes the need for husbands to treat their wives with care and respect. Both husbands and wives are equal heirs of God's grace and eternal life. This highlights the spiritual equality and shared inheritance in Christ.

The verse concludes with a reminder that how husbands treat their wives can impact their spiritual lives. Dishonoring or mistreating one's wife can hinder the husband's prayers. This verse underscores the importance of mutual respect, understanding, and honor in a marriage, reflecting the love and grace that God extends to all believers.

6. What does verse fourteen mean?

The verse acknowledges that believers might suffer for doing what is right in God's eyes. This suffering is not a result of wrongdoing but rather for standing up for one's faith and principles. Despite the suffering, believers are blessed. This blessing is not necessarily about finding joy in the suffering itself but recognizing that enduring such trials can lead to spiritual growth and favor with God. The verse encourages believers not to fear or be troubled by those who oppose or persecute them. Instead, they should remain steadfast and confident in their faith. 1 Peter 3:14 reassures believers that suffering for doing what is right is a noble and blessed condition, and they should not be intimidated or troubled by opposition.

7. What is the defense described in verse fifteen?

Believers are encouraged to revere Christ as Lord in their hearts. This means recognizing His holiness and authority in their lives. Christians should always be ready to explain the reason for their hope and faith. This involves being knowledgeable about their beliefs and being able to articulate them clearly. When sharing their faith or defending their beliefs, Christians are instructed to do so with gentleness and respect. This approach helps maintain a positive witness and fosters constructive dialogue. 1 Peter 3:15 encourages believers to be prepared to share their faith thoughtfully and respectfully, while keeping Christ at the center of their lives.

8. What does verse seventeen mean?

The verse emphasizes that if suffering is inevitable; it is better to suffer for doing what is right and good in God's eyes rather than for doing wrong. The phrase "if it is God's will" acknowledges that sometimes suffering is part of God's plan for our lives. This suffering can serve a greater purpose, such as strengthening our faith or serving as a testimony to others. The verse contrasts suffering for good versus suffering for evil. Suffering for good is seen as honorable and aligned with God's will, whereas suffering for evil is a consequence of wrongdoing. This verse encourages believers to remain steadfast in doing good, even if it leads to suffering, as this aligns with God's will and brings greater spiritual benefit.[10]

9. Is there a requirement to suffer like Yeshua did? (v. 18)

When becoming a Christian in the early church the individual could go through some suffering. That suffering would be if the person had a government job, they

---

[10] 1. The meaning of 1 peter 3:17 explained, accessed July 31, 2024,
https://www.scripturespeaks.org/verse/1+peter+3%3A17.

would lose it immediately. Early Christians had a come together in communes to protect themselves in the persecution that occurred, especially from the Roman government. To stop people from leaving the faith, the church connected the suffering of the believers to the suffering of Yeshua. Their prime aim was to not let anyone leave the faith.

10. Did Yeshua go to Hades? (v. 19)

Ancient Hebrews believed that hell was a place for departed souls that were awaiting the final resurrection, the Tikkun. It was a place of silence and inactivity and was supposed to be somewhere under the ground. The people that were in hell could not reach out to the forces of the universe and communicate with the God of Israel. Therefore, those souls were in hell were cut off from the rest of humanity and from the living God. It is believed that the gates of hell were locked so tight that there was no way to escape. Yeshua taught that his followers not only defied the mysterious realm of hell and conquered death, but he also gave his disciples in the church the assurance that they will not be held at any time in hell. The church professes that Yeshua while he was in hell preached of departed souls, so they might also share in his resurrection.

11. Is a spirit considered in prison Hades? (v. 19)

When the spirit was sent to Hades, it was imprisoned until the general resurrection at the end of time when the great Tikkun would occur.

12. Who were the eight people brought safely through the water? (v. 20)

The eight people who entered the ark were Noah, his wife, his three sons, and three daughter-in-law's.

13. What does "in the waters" mean in verse twenty?

This means that the eight people in the ark were saved in the waters by the ark.

14. How does baptism relate to Noah's ark? (v. 21)

The author is making a comparison between a personal baptism in which one is saved by water and the Noah's Ark story.

15. Does the appeal to God include a promise? (v. 21)

This depends on which expression of Christianity you believe in. According to Catholicism, receiving baptism in the name of Yeshua includes a promise from God but also a personal promise to God. In Lutheranism, it is believed that God gives the gift of baptism freely and the person owes absolutely nothing.

16. How do we connect to God through the resurrection of Yeshua? (v. 22)

The resurrection of Yeshua is believed to offer freedom from sin. One is forgiven for all sins when one comes to accept Yeshua. In this way, one is connected to God through Yeshua's resurrection.

Culture Section

Questioning the passage

1. Why is braiding your hair unacceptable? (v. 3)

In the Greco-Roman culture of the time, elaborate hairstyles, often adorned with gold and pearls, were a display of wealth and social status. Paul, in his letters, emphasized modesty and humility, encouraging women to focus on inner beauty and godliness rather than outward appearances. So, it was not the act of braiding hair that was the issue, but the potential for such styles to be associated with vanity and extravagance.

2. Why is there a restriction on jewelry and fine clothing? (v. 3)

The restriction on braided hair being a display of wealth and social status is addressed with jewelry and fine clothing. All the members of a congregation were supposed to be equal. Therefore, they should dress equally. In the early church houses, everyone shared everything. A person withholding their wealth would be frowned upon.

Thoughts

This chapter comprises more exhortations on how one is to live a Christian life.

Language

Peshitta	New American Standard 1995
1Peter 4:1 If then the Messiah hath suffered for you in the flesh, do ye also arm yourselves with the same mind: for every one that is dead in his body, hath ceased from all sins, 2 that he may no longer be alive to the lusts of men, while he is in the body, but [only] to do the pleasure of God. 3 For the time that is past was enough, when ye wrought the pleasure of the profane, in dissoluteness, and in ebriety, and in lasciviousness, and in revelling, and in the worship of demons. 4 And lo, they now wonder, and reproach you, because ye revel not with them in the same former dissoluteness; 5 who must give account to God, who is to judge the living and the dead. 6 For on this account the announcement is made also to the dead, that they may be judged as persons in the flesh, and may live according to God in the spirit. 7 But the end of all things approacheth: therefore be sober, and be wakeful for prayer. 8 And above all things, have fervent love one towards another; for love covereth a multitude of sins. 9 And be ye compassionate to strangers, without murmuring. 10 And let each of you minister to his associates the gift which he hath received from God; as being good stewards of the manifold grace of God. 11 Whoever will speak, let him speak as the word of God: and whoever will minister, as of the ability that God hath given him: so that in all ye do, God may be glorified,	1 Peter 4:1 Therefore, since [a]Christ has [1]suffered in the flesh, [b]arm yourselves also with the same purpose, because [c]he who has [1]suffered in the flesh has ceased from sin, 2 [a]so as to live [b]the rest of the time in the flesh no longer for the lusts of men, but for the [c]will of God. 3 For [a]the time already past is sufficient *for you* to have carried out the desire of the Gentiles, [1b]having pursued a course of sensuality, lusts, drunkenness, carousing, drinking parties and [2]abominable idolatries. 4 In *all* this, they are surprised that you do not run with *them* into the same excesses of [a]dissipation, and they [b]malign *you;* 5 but they will give account to Him who is ready to judge [a]the living and the dead. 6 For [a]the gospel has for this purpose been [1]preached even to those who are dead, that though they are judged in the flesh as men, they may live in the spirit according to *the will of* God. 1Peter 4:7 [a]The end of all things [1]is near; therefore, [b]be of sound judgment and sober *spirit* for the purpose of [2]prayer. 8 Above all, [a]keep fervent in your love for one another, because [b]love covers a multitude of sins. 9 [a]Be hospitable to one another without [b]complaint. 10 [a]As each one has received a *special* gift, employ it in serving one another as good [b]stewards of the manifold grace of God. 11 [a]Whoever speaks, *is to do so* [1]as one who is speaking

through Jesus the Messiah; to whom belongeth glory, and honor, for ever and ever. Amen. 12 My beloved, be not dismayed at the trials that befall you, as if some strange thing had come upon you; for these things are for your probation. 13 But rejoice, that ye participate in the sufferings of the Messiah, that so ye may also rejoice and exult at the revelation of his glory. 14 And if ye are reproached on account of the name of the Messiah, happy are ye: for the glorious Spirit of God resteth upon you. 15 Only let none of you suffer, as a murderer, or as a thief, or as an evil-doer. 16 But if he suffer as a Christian, let him not be ashamed; but let him glorify God on account of this name. 17 For it is the time when judgment will commence with the house of God: and if it commence with us, what will be the end of those who obey not the gospel of God? 18 And if the righteous scarcely liveth, where will the ungodly and the sinner be found! 19 Wherefore, let them who suffer according to the pleasure of God, commend their souls to him in well doing, as to a faithful Creator.

the [b]utterances of God; whoever serves *is to do so* as one who is serving [2a]by the strength which God supplies; so that [d]in all things God may be glorified through Jesus Christ, [e]to whom belongs the glory and dominion forever and ever. Amen.

1Peter 4:12 [a]Beloved, do not be surprised at the [b]fiery ordeal among you, which comes upon you for your testing, as though some strange thing were happening to you; 13 but to the degree that you [a]share the sufferings of Christ, keep on rejoicing, so that also at the [b]revelation of His glory [c]you may rejoice with exultation. 14 If you are reviled [1a]for the name of Christ, [b]you are blessed, [c]because the Spirit of glory and of God rests on you. 15 Make sure that [a]none of you suffers as a murderer, or thief, or evildoer, or a [1b]troublesome meddler; 16 but if *anyone suffers* as a [a]Christian, he is not to be ashamed, but is to [b]glorify God in this name. 17 For *it is* time for judgment [a]to begin [1]with [b]the household of God; and if *it* [c]begins with us first, what *will be* the outcome for those [d]who do not obey the [e]gospel of God? 18 [a]AND IF IT IS WITH DIFFICULTY THAT THE RIGHTEOUS IS SAVED, [1]WHAT WILL BECOME OF THE [b]GODLESS MAN AND THE SINNER? 19 Therefore, those also who suffer according to [a]the will of God shall entrust their souls to a faithful Creator in doing what is right.

1Peter 4:1
[1]I.e. suffered death
[a]1 Pet 2:21
[b]Eph 6:13
[c]Rom 6:7

1Peter 4:2
[a]Rom 6:2; Col 3:3
[b]1 Pet 1:14
[c]Mark 3:35

1Peter 4:3
[1]Lit *having gone in*
[2]Lit *lawless*
[a]1 Cor 12:2
[b]Rom 13:13; Eph 2:2; 4:17ff

1Peter 4:4
[a]Eph 5:18
[b]1 Pet 3:16

1Peter 4:5
[a]Acts 10:42; Rom 14:9; 2 Tim 4:1

1Peter 4:6
[1]I.e. preached in their lifetimes
[a]1 Pet 3:18

1Peter 4:7
[1]Lit *has come near*
[2]Lit *prayers*
[a]Rom 13:11; Heb 9:26; James 5:8; 1 John 2:18
[b]1 Pet 1:13

1Peter 4:8
[a]1 Pet 1:22
[b]Prov 10:12; 1 Cor 13:4ff; James 5:20

1Peter 4:9
[a]1 Tim 3:2; Heb 13:2
[b]Phil 2:14

1Peter 4:10
[a]Rom 12:6f
[b]1 Cor 4:1

1Peter 4:11
[1]Lit *as utterances*
[2]Lit *from*
[a]1 Thess 2:4; Titus 2:1, 15; Heb 13:7
[b]Acts 7:38
[c]Eph 1:19; 6:10
[d]1 Cor 10:31; 1 Pet 2:12
[e]Rom 11:36; 1 Pet 5:11; Rev 1:6; 5:13

1Peter 4:12
[a]1 Pet 2:11
[b]1 Pet 1:6f

1Peter 4:13
[a]Rom 8:17; 2 Cor 1:5; 4:10; Phil 3:10
[b]2 Tim 2:12
[c]1 Pet 1:7; 5:1

1Peter 4:14
[1]Lit *in*
[a]John 15:21; Heb 11:26; 1 Pet 4:16
[b]Matt 5:11; Luke 6:22; Acts 5:41
[c]2 Cor 4:10f, 16

1Peter 4:15
[1]Lit *one who oversees others' affairs*
[a]1 Pet 2:19f; 3:17
[b]1 Thess 4:11; 2 Thess 3:11; 1 Tim 5:13

1Peter 4:16
[a]Acts 5:41; 28:22; James 2:7
[b]1 Pet 4:11

1Peter 4:17
[1]Lit *from*
[a]Jer 25:29; Ezek 9:6; Amos 3:2
[b]1 Tim 3:15; Heb 3:6; 1 Pet 2:5
[c]Rom 2:9
[d]2 Thess 1:8
[e]Rom 1:1

1Peter 4:18
[1]Lit *where will appear*
[a]Prov 11:31; Luke 23:31
[b]1 Tim 1:9

1Peter 4:19
[a]1 Pet 3:17

Koine Greek

1Peter 4:1   Χριστοῦ οὖν παθόντος ὑπὲρ ἡμῶν σαρκί, καὶ ὑμεῖς τὴν αὐτὴν ἔννοιαν ὁπλίσασθε· ὅτι ὁ παθὼν ἐν σαρκί, πέπαυται ἁμαρτίας· 2 εἰς τὸ μηκέτι ἀνθρώπων ἐπιθυμίαις, ἀλλὰ θελήματι θεοῦ τὸν ἐπίλοιπον ἐν σαρκὶ βιῶσαι χρόνον. 3 Ἀρκετὸς γὰρ ⸂ ἡμῖν ⸃ ὁ παρεληλυθὼς χρόνος τοῦ βίου τὸ θέλημα τῶν ἐθνῶν κατεργάσασθαι, πεπορευμένους ἐν ἀσελγείαις, ἐπιθυμίαις, οἰνοφλυγίαις, κώμοις, πότοις, καὶ ἀθεμίτοις εἰδωλολατρείαις· 4 ἐν ᾧ ξενίζονται, μὴ συντρεχόντων ὑμῶν εἰς τὴν αὐτὴν τῆς ἀσωτίας ἀνάχυσιν, βλασφημοῦντες· 5 οἳ ἀποδώσουσιν λόγον τῷ ἑτοίμως ἔχοντι κρῖναι ζῶντας καὶ νεκρούς. 6 Εἰς τοῦτο γὰρ καὶ νεκροῖς εὐηγγελίσθη, ἵνα κριθῶσιν μὲν κατὰ ἀνθρώπους σαρκί, ζῶσιν δὲ κατὰ θεὸν πνεύματι.

1Peter 4:7   Πάντων δὲ τὸ τέλος ἤγγικεν· σωφρονήσατε οὖν καὶ νήψατε εἰς τὰς προσευχάς· 8 πρὸ πάντων δὲ τὴν εἰς ἑαυτοὺς ἀγάπην ἐκτενῆ ἔχοντες, ὅτι ἀγάπη καλύψει πλῆθος ἁμαρτιῶν· 9 φιλόξενοι εἰς ἀλλήλους ἄνευ γογγυσμῶν· 10 ἕκαστος καθὼς ἔλαβεν χάρισμα, εἰς ἑαυτοὺς αὐτὸ διακονοῦντες, ὡς καλοὶ οἰκονόμοι ποικίλης χάριτος θεοῦ· 11 εἴ τις λαλεῖ, ὡς λόγια θεοῦ· εἴ τις διακονεῖ, ὡς ἐξ ἰσχύος ὡς χορηγεῖ ὁ θεός· ἵνα ἐν πᾶσιν δοξάζηται ὁ θεὸς διὰ Ἰησοῦ χριστοῦ, ᾧ ἐστιν ἡ δόξα καὶ τὸ κράτος εἰς τοὺς αἰῶνας τῶν αἰώνων. Ἀμήν.

1Peter 4:12   Ἀγαπητοί, μὴ ξενίζεσθε τῇ ἐν ὑμῖν πυρώσει πρὸς πειρασμὸν ὑμῖν γινομένη, ὡς ξένου ὑμῖν συμβαίνοντος· 13 ἀλλὰ καθὸ κοινωνεῖτε τοῖς τοῦ χριστοῦ παθήμασιν, χαίρετε, ἵνα καὶ ἐν τῇ ἀποκαλύψει τῆς δόξης αὐτοῦ χαρῆτε ἀγαλλιώμενοι. 14 Εἰ ὀνειδίζεσθε ἐν ὀνόματι χριστοῦ, μακάριοι· ὅτι τὸ τῆς δόξης καὶ τὸ τοῦ θεοῦ πνεῦμα ἐφ᾽ ὑμᾶς ἀναπαύεται· κατὰ μὲν αὐτοὺς βλασφημεῖται, κατὰ δὲ ὑμᾶς δοξάζεται. 15 Μὴ γάρ τις ὑμῶν πασχέτω ὡς φονεύς, ἢ κλέπτης, ἢ κακοποιός, ἢ ὡς ἀλλοτριοεπίσκοπος· 16 εἰ δὲ ὡς χριστιανός, μὴ αἰσχυνέσθω, δοξαζέτω δὲ τὸν θεὸν ἐν τῷ μέρει τούτῳ. 17 Ὅτι ὁ καιρὸς τοῦ ἄρξασθαι τὸ κρίμα ἀπὸ τοῦ οἴκου τοῦ θεοῦ. εἰ δὲ πρῶτον ἀφ᾽ ἡμῶν, τί τὸ τέλος τῶν ἀπειθούντων τῷ τοῦ θεοῦ εὐαγγελίῳ; 18 Καὶ εἰ ὁ δίκαιος μόλις σώζεται, ὁ ἀσεβὴς καὶ ἁμαρτωλὸς ποῦ φανεῖται; 19 Ὥστε καὶ οἱ πάσχοντες κατὰ τὸ θέλημα τοῦ θεοῦ, ὡς πιστῷ κτίστῃ παρατιθέσθωσαν τὰς ψυχὰς αὐτῶν ἐν ἀγαθοποιΐᾳ.

Language

Process of Discovery

Linguistics Section

Linguistic Structure

[Yeshua's suffering] 1 Therefore, since ^aChrist has ¹suffered in the flesh, ^barm yourselves also with the same purpose, because ^che who has ¹suffered in the flesh has ceased from sin, 2 ^aso as to live ^bthe rest of the time in the flesh no longer for the lusts of men, but for the ^cwill of God.

[Time to Emulate Yeshua] 3 For ^athe time already past is sufficient *for you* to have carried out the desire of the Gentiles, ^{1b}having pursued a course of sensuality, lusts, drunkenness, carousing, drinking parties and ²abominable idolatries. 4 In *all* this, they are surprised that you do not run with *them* into the same excesses of ^adissipation, and they ^bmalign *you;* 5 but they will give account to Him who is ready to judge ^athe living and the dead. 6 For ^athe gospel has for this purpose been ¹preached even to those who are dead, that though they are judged in the flesh as men, they may live in the spirit according to *the will of* God.

[Prepare for Apocolypse] 7 ^aThe end of all things ¹is near; therefore, ^bbe of sound judgment and sober *spirit* for the purpose of ²prayer. 8 Above all, ^akeep fervent in your love for one another, because ^blove covers a multitude of sins. 9 ^aBe hospitable to one another without ^bcomplaint. 10 ^aAs each one has received a *special* gift, employ it in serving one another as good ^bstewards of the manifold grace of God. 11 ^aWhoever speaks, *is to do so* ¹as one who is speaking the ^butterances of God; whoever serves *is to do so* as one who is serving ^{2c}by the strength which God supplies; so that ^din all things God may be glorified through Jesus Christ, ^eto whom belongs the glory and dominion forever and ever. Amen.

[Upcoming tests of faith] 12 ^aBeloved, do not be surprised at the ^bfiery ordeal among you, which comes upon you for your testing, as though some strange thing were happening to you; 13 but to the degree that you ^ashare the sufferings of Christ, keep on rejoicing, so that also at the ^brevelation of His glory ^cyou may rejoice with exultation. 14 If you are reviled ^{1a}for the name of Christ, ^byou are blessed, ^cbecause the Spirit of glory and of God rests on you. 15 Make sure that ^anone of you suffers as a murderer, or thief, or evildoer, or a ^{1b}troublesome meddler; 16 but if *anyone suffers* as a ^aChristian, he is not to be ashamed, but is to ^bglorify God in this name. 17 For *it is* time for judgment ^ato begin ¹with ^bthe household of God; and if *it* ^cbegins with us first, what *will be* the outcome for those ^dwho do not obey the ^egospel of God? 18 ^aAND IF IT IS WITH

DIFFICULTY THAT THE RIGHTEOUS IS SAVED, [1]WHAT WILL BECOME OF THE [b]GODLESS MAN AND THE SINNER? 19 Therefore, those also who suffer according to [a]the will of God shall entrust their souls to a faithful Creator in doing what is right.

Discussion

This chapter reminds people to behave as Yeshua has instructed.

Questioning the Passage

1. What does verse one and two mean?

   The author is saying that each member of the congregation could suffer in the same way that Yeshua did. They needed to prepare themselves for the possibility of being arrested by either the Romans or Jews and crucified.

2. How do you preach the gospel to the dead? (v. 6)

   Preaching the gospel to the dead refers to the belief that the gospel message of Yeshua's death and resurrection is meant for everyone, even those who have died. There is no definitive definition offered how to accomplish this.

3. Why did the author believe the apocalypse was soon approaching? (v. 7)

   This was a tradition that originated when Paul converted the Mithras Churches into Yeshua Churches. The Mithras cult believed that the messiah Mithras was going to return to complete his work. It also covered the point that when Yeshua was on earth all of the points of the messianic tradition did not come to pass.

4. How does love cover a multitude of sins? (v. 8)

Christian tradition says that Yeshua's death covered the sins of the past, present and future. It is Yeshua's love for humanity that spreads this blanket of forgiveness.

5. How does one know what the special gift from God is? (v. 10)

A special gift from God is something that you cannot receive from another person.

6. What does it mean to share the suffering of Yeshua? (v. 12)

Those who preach the gospel of Yeshua can face a similar suffering as Yeshua did. In many places in the world today, one would be killed for mentioning Yeshua. During the first 300 years of Christianity, just saying you are a Christian could get you persecuted and possibly killed.

7. What is the revelation of Yeshua? (v. 13)

This is the apocalypse.

8. What does verse sixteen mean?

This means by following Yeshua's way, one is made holy.

9. Why is the household of God being held accountable first? (v. 17)

Those who have come to believe and have faith in Yeshua will be held accountable as to whether or not they actually followed Yeshua's ways.

Verse Comparison of citations or proof text

1. **5** ^aYou ¹younger men, likewise, ^bbe subject to *your* elders; and all of you, clothe yourselves with ^chumility toward one another, because ^dGOD IS OPPOSED TO THE PROUD, BUT HE GIVES GRACE TO THE HUMBLE.

5 ^aYou ¹younger men, likewise, ^bbe subject to *your* elders; and all of you, clothe yourselves with ^chumility toward one another, because ^dGOD IS OPPOSED TO THE PROUD, BUT HE GIVES GRACE TO THE HUMBLE.

Thoughts

The chapter emphasizes that we need to go out and tell people about Yeshua. When we do that we will be tested of our true faith because it will be people going to try to stop us.

Language

Peshitta	New American Standard 1995
1Pet. 5:1 And I, an Elder, your associate, and a witness of the sufferings of the Messiah, and a participator in his glory which is to be revealed, entreat the Elders who are among you: **2** Feed ye the flock of God which is committed to you: have care [for it], spiritually; not from compulsion, but voluntarily; not for base gain, but with all your heart; **3** not as lords of the flock, but so as to be a good example for them: **4** that when the chief shepherd shall be revealed, ye may receive from him a crown of glory that fadeth not. **5** And ye juniors submit yourselves to your seniors; and clothe yourselves, stringently, with lowliness of mind one towards another; because God resisteth them who exalt themselves, and giveth grace to the humble. **6** Humble yourselves, therefore, under the powerful hand of God: and it will exalt you in due time. **7** And cast all your solicitude upon God; for he careth for you. **8** Be sober and guarded, because Satan your adversary, like a lion, roareth, and goeth about, and seeketh whom he may devour. **9** Therefore resist him, being steadfast in the faith: and know ye, that the same sufferings befall your brethren that are in the world. **10** Now it is the God of grace, who hath called us to his eternal glory by Jesus the Messiah, that hath given us, while we sustain these light afflictions, to be strengthened, and confirmed, and established by him for ever: **11** to whom be	**1Pet. 5:1** *a*Therefore, I exhort the elders among you, as *your* *b*fellow elder and *c*witness of the sufferings of Christ, and a *d*partaker also of the glory that is to be revealed, **2** shepherd *a*the flock of God among you, exercising oversight *b*not under compulsion, but voluntarily, according to *the will of* God; and *c*not for sordid gain, but with eagerness; **3** nor yet as *d*lording it over *1*those allotted to your charge, but *2*proving to be *b*examples to the flock. **4** And when the Chief *a*Shepherd appears, you will receive the *b*unfading *1c*crown of glory. **5** *a*You younger men, likewise, *b*be subject to *your* elders; and all of you, clothe yourselves with *c*humility toward one another, for *d*GOD IS OPPOSED TO THE PROUD, BUT GIVES GRACE TO THE HUMBLE. **1Pet. 5:6** Therefore *a*humble yourselves under the mighty hand of God, that He may exalt you at the proper time, **7** casting all your *a*anxiety on Him, because He cares for you. **8** *a*Be of sober *spirit,* *b*be on the alert. Your adversary, *c*the devil, prowls around like a roaring *d*lion, seeking someone to devour. **9** *1a*But resist him, *b*firm in *your* faith, knowing that *c*the same experiences of suffering are being accomplished by your *2*brethren who are in the world. **10** After you have suffered *a*for a little while, the *b*God of all grace, who *c*called you to His *d*eternal glory in

glory, and power, and honor, for ever and ever. Amen. **12** These as I account [them] few [things], I have written to you by Sylvanus, a faithful brother. And I would persuade, and would testify, that this is the true grace of God, this in which ye stand. **13** The elect church which is in Babylon, saluteth you; also Mark, my son. **14** Salute ye one another with a holy kiss. Peace be with you all, who are in the Messiah. Amen.

Christ, will Himself *perfect*, *confirm*, strengthen *and* establish you. **11** *To Him be* dominion forever and ever. Amen.

1Pet. 5:12 Through *Silvanus, our faithful brother [1](for so I regard *him*), *I have written to you briefly, exhorting and testifying that this is *the true grace of God. *Stand firm in it! **13** She who is in Babylon, chosen together with you, sends you greetings, and *so does* my son, *Mark. **14** *Greet one another with a kiss of love.

*Peace be to you all who are in Christ.

1Peter 5:1
*a*Acts 11:30
*b*2 John 1; 3 John 1
*c*Luke 24:48; Heb 12:1
*d*1 Pet 1:5, 7; 4:13; Rev 1:9

1Peter 5:2
*a*John 21:16; Acts 20:28
*b*Philem 14
*c*1 Tim 3:8

1Peter 5:3
*1*Lit *the allotments*
*2*Or *becoming*
*a*Ezek 34:4; Matt 20:25f
*b*John 13:15; Phil 3:17; 1 Thess 1:7; 2 Thess 3:9; 1 Tim 4:12; Titus 2:7

1Peter 5:4
*1*Lit *wreath*
*a*1 Pet 2:25
*b*1 Pet 1:4
*c*1 Cor 9:25

1Peter 5:5
*a*Luke 22:26; 1 Tim 5:1
*b*Eph 5:21
*c*1 Pet 3:8
*d*Prov 3:34; James 4:6

1Peter 5:6
*a*Matt 23:12; Luke 14:11; 18:14; James 4:10

1Peter 5:7
*a*Ps 55:22; Matt 6:25

1Peter 5:8
*a*1 Pet 1:13

*b*Matt 24:42
*c*James 4:7
*d*2 Tim 4:17

1Peter 5:9
[1]Lit *whom resist*
[2]Lit *brotherhood*
*a*James 4:7
*b*Col 2:5
*c*Acts 14:22

1Peter 5:10
*a*1 Pet 1:6
*b*1 Pet 4:10
*c*1 Cor 1:9; 1 Thess 2:12
*d*2 Cor 4:17; 2 Tim 2:10
*e*1 Cor 1:10; Heb 13:21
*f*Rom 16:25; 2 Thess 2:17; 3:3

1Peter 5:11
*a*Rom 11:36; 1 Pet 4:11

1Peter 5:12
[1]Lit *(as I consider)*
*a*2 Cor 1:19
*b*Heb 13:22
*c*Acts 11:23; 1 Pet 1:13; 4:10
*d*1 Cor 15:1

1Peter 5:13
*a*Acts 12:12, 25; 15:37, 39; Col 4:10; Philem 24

1Peter 5:14
*a*Rom 16:16
*b*Eph 6:23

Koine Greek

1Pet. 5:1   Πρεσβυτερους τους εν υμιν παρακαλω ο συμπρεσβυτερος και μαρτυς των του Χριστου παθηματων, ο και της μελλουσης αποκαλυπτεσθαι δοξης κοινωνος· ² ποιμανατε το εν υμιν ποιμνιον του θεου επισκοπουντες μη αναγκαστως αλλ' εκουσιως κατα θεον, μηδε αισχροκερδως αλλα προθυμως, ³ μηδ' ως κατακυριευοντες των κληρων αλλα τυποι γινομενοι του ποιμνιου· ⁴ και φανερωθεντος του αρχιποιμενος κομιεισθε τον αμαραντινον της δοξης στεφανον. ⁵ ομοιως, νεωτεροι, υποταγητε πρεσβυτεροις· παντες δε αλληλοις την ταπεινοφροσυνην εγκομβωσασθε, οτι ο θεος *υπερηφανοις αντιτασσεται, ταπεινοις δε διδωσιν χαριν.*

1Pet. 5:6   Ταπεινωθητε ουν υπο την κραταιαν χειρα του θεου, ινα υμας υψωση εν καιρω, ⁷ πασαν την μεριμναν υμων επιριψαντες επ' αυτον, οτι αυτω μελει περι υμων. ⁸ νηψατε, γρηγορησατε. ο αντιδικος υμων διαβολος *ως λεων ωρυομενος* περιπατει ζητων τινα καταπιειν· ⁹ ω αντιστητε στερεοι τη πιστει ειδοτες τα αυτα των παθηματων τη εν κοσμω υμων αδελφοτητι επιτελεισθαι. ¹⁰ ο δε θεος πασης χαριτος, ο καλεσας υμας εις την αιωνιον αυτου δοξαν εν Χριστω ολιγον παθοντας αυτος καταρτισει, στηριξει, σθενωσει, θεμελιωσει. ¹¹ αυτω το κρατος εις τους αιωνας, αμην.

1Pet. 5:12   Δια Σιλουανου υμιν του πιστου αδελφου, ως λογιζομαι, δι' ολιγων εγραψα παρακαλων και επιμαρτυρων ταυτην ειναι αληθη χαριν του θεου εις ην στητε. ¹³ ασπαζεται υμας η εν Βαβυλωνι συνεκλεκτη και Μαρκος ο υιος μου. ¹⁴ ασπασασθε αλληλους εν φιληματι αγαπης.

Ειρηνη υμιν πασιν τοις εν Χριστω.

Language

Process of Discovery

Linguistics Section

Linguistic Structure

[Exhortation] 1   *Therefore, I exhort the elders among you, as *your* *fellow elder and *witness of the sufferings of Christ, and a *partaker also of the glory that is to be revealed, **2** shepherd *the flock of God among you, exercising oversight *not under compulsion, but voluntarily, according to *the will of* God; and *not for sordid gain, but with eagerness; **3** nor yet as *lording it over [1]those allotted to your charge, but [2]proving to be *examples to the flock. **4** And when the Chief *Shepherd appears, you will receive the *unfading [1c]crown of glory. **5** *You younger men, likewise, *be subject to *your* elders; and all of you, clothe yourselves with *humility toward one another, for *GOD IS OPPOSED TO THE PROUD, BUT GIVES GRACE TO THE HUMBLE.

[Exhortation] 6   Therefore *humble yourselves under the mighty hand of God, that He may exalt you at the proper time, **7** casting all your *anxiety on Him, because He cares for you. **8** *Be of sober *spirit,* *be on the alert. Your adversary, *the devil, prowls around like a roaring *lion, seeking someone to devour. **9** [1]*But resist him, *firm in *your* faith, knowing that *the same experiences of suffering are being accomplished by your [2]brethren who are in the world. **10** After you have suffered *for a little while, the *God of all grace, who *called you to His *eternal glory in Christ, will Himself *perfect, *confirm, strengthen *and* establish you. **11** *To Him *be* dominion forever and ever. Amen.

[Closing] 12   Through *Silvanus, our faithful brother [1](for so I regard *him*), *I have written to you briefly, exhorting and testifying that this is *the true grace of God. *Stand firm in it! **13** She who is in Babylon, chosen together with you, sends you greetings, and *so does* my son, *Mark. **14** *Greet one another with a kiss of love. *Peace be to you all who are in Christ.

Discussion

This chapter continues with exhortations to the people.

Questioning the Passage

1. What is the position of elder in the church? (v. 1)

The term elder means minister or presbyter. Their main responsibility was to take care of bringing new followers into the fold. They needed to teach the new followers the religion of Jesus Christ. In the near East such offices were held by elderly men whom the young people honored and respected. The Jewish people appointed elderly men to high offices to attend to the needs of the people. The elders would lay their hands upon animals that were being offered for sins. In the Jewish religion, the elders were not priests, nor were they permitted performing any priestly functions. Their work was mostly judicial and administrative. In ancient days, the government and the religion were one.

The elders who were appointed by the apostles were not priests but rather ministers to the people. They were to help the current community and new followers to understand what the religion of Yeshua was all about. Jewish followers of Yeshua were free to worship as they pleased. Most of them continued with their Hebraic practices.

The elders were selected from among men who were noted for their piety, humility, kindness, and who could serve freely. They would be like shepherds to the community.

2. Who was the Chief Shepherd? (v. 4)

The Chief Shepherd is Jesus Christ. The tradition of Jesus' return was anticipated in Judaism and in the Mithras cult. The Zohar discusses the two messiahs because of the wording of Zecharia 9:9 which says that the messiah will return riding on a donkey and a colt. The Mithras cult believed that Mithras would return.

3. What is the unfading crown of glory? (v. 4)

The phrase "unfading crown of glory" is often associated with the reward believers will receive in heaven. This phrase emphasizes the eternal nature of the reward. It will never fade, tarnish, or disappear. The symbolism is victory, honor, and royalty. It represents the ultimate triumph over sin and suffering. Glory refers to the splendor, majesty, and brilliance of God's presence. It signifies the fullness of joy and satisfaction that believers will experience in heaven.

Therefore, the "unfading crown of glory" is a metaphor for the eternal reward that awaits those who remain faithful to God. It's a promise of ultimate joy, honor, and closeness to God in the future.

4. What does it mean to caste all your anxieties on Him? (v. 7)

The author was telling the followers that they could count on Yeshua to take care of matters for they. If one places a full trust in Yeshua it is believed that he can take care of all matters. Thus, there is no reason to be anxious about anything.

5. What does verse ten mean?

This sets the stage by reminding us of God's immense grace and mercy. He is the source of all that is good and loving.

"...who hath called us unto his eternal glory by Christ Jesus." This emphasizes our destiny in Christ. God has chosen us to share in His eternal glory, a future filled with joy and perfection.

"...after that ye have suffered a while..." This phrase acknowledges that the path to this glory may involve trials and suffering.

"...make you perfect, establish strengthen, settle you." This phrase is the promise of God's help. He will complete what He started in us, making us strong, and secure in our faith, even through difficulties.

This verse offers comfort and encouragement. Even when facing hardship, God is with us. He will sustain us and bring us to ultimate victory. Our suffering is temporary, but our eternal glory is certain.

6. What is a holy kiss? (v. 14)

   This phrase is a gesture of greeting and affection among Christians.

7. What does it mean to be in Christ? (v. 14)

   A person is "in Christ" then said person is following the ways Jesus tells to live. This "manual of life" can be found in the Gospels.

Verse Comparison of citations or proof text

1. 5 *a*You younger men, likewise, *b*be subject to *your* elders; and all of you, clothe yourselves with *c*humility toward one another, for *d*GOD IS OPPOSED TO THE PROUD, the new followers to adhere to the Bible GIVES GRACE TO THE HUMBLE.

Biblical Personalities

1. Silvanus

   Silvanus is believed to be the same person as Silas, a prominent figure in the early Christian church. He was a companion of Paul and a fellow missionary. They traveled together, preached the gospel, and faced persecution. Silvanus/Silas was a faithful and influential figure in the early church. He played a key role in spreading the gospel, supporting Paul's ministry, and contributing to the development of Christian doctrine.

2. Mark

   Peter refers to Mark as "Marcus my son," indicating a close familial bond. It's possible Mark was a younger Christian whom Peter took under his wing and mentored.

Thoughts

This chapter is a continuation of exhortations that are found in previous chapters.. To achieve salvation and eternal life, one must follow Yeshua. A person's words and actions tell the story of whether the person believes in Yeshua.

Introduction to 2 Peter Epistle

Most scholars believe this letter was written between 120 to 130 CE and definitely not by Peter. They also suggest that was probably written to a general audience of eastern Mediterranean Christians.

The author of the epistle warns the people against false teachings that came from different expressions of Christianity. One area concentrated on is the second coming of Yeshua and the day of judgment. The people were tired of awaiting the second coming because Paul told him it would happen before his death, and they were just waiting. On the day of judgment, the world was going to change, and they would no longer be persecuted.

2 Peter Chapter One

Language

Peshitta	New American Standard 1995
2Peter 1:1 Simon Peter, a servant and legate of Jesus the Messiah, to those who have obtained equally precious faith with us, through the righteousness of Our Lord and Redeemer, Jesus the Messiah; 2 May grace and peace abound to you through the recognition of our Lord Jesus the Messiah, 3 as the giver to us of all things that be of the power of God, unto life and the fear of God, through the recognition of him who hath called us unto his own glory and moral excellence: 4 wherein he hath given you very great and precious promises; that by them ye might become partakers of the nature of God, while ye flee from the corruptions of the lusts that are in the world. 5 And, while ye apply all diligence in the matter, add to your faith moral excellence; and to moral excellence, knowledge; 6 and to knowledge, perseverance; and to perseverance, patience; and to patience, the fear of God; 7 and to the fear of God, sympathy with the brotherhood; and to sympathy with the brotherhood, love. 8 For, while these are found in you, and abounding, they render you not slothful, and not unfruitful, in the recognition of our Lord Jesus the Messiah. 9 For he, in whom these things are not found, is blind and seeth not, and hath forgotten the purgation of his former sins. 10 And therefore, my brethren, be ye exceedingly diligent to make your calling	2Peter 1:1 [1]Simon Peter, a [a]bond-servant and [b]apostle of Jesus Christ, To those who have received [c]a faith of the same [2]kind as ours, [3]by [d]the righteousness of [e]our God and Savior, Jesus Christ: 2 [a]Grace and peace be multiplied to you in [b]the knowledge of God and of Jesus our Lord; 3 seeing that His [a]divine power has granted to us everything pertaining to life and godliness, through the true [b]knowledge of Him who [c]called us [1]by His own glory and [2]excellence. 4 [1]For by these He has granted to us His precious and magnificent [a]promises, so that by them you may become [b]partakers of *the* divine nature, having [c]escaped the [d]corruption that is in [e]the world by lust. 5 Now for this very reason also, applying all diligence, in your faith [a]supply [b]moral [1]excellence, and in *your* moral excellence, [c]knowledge, 6 and in *your* knowledge, [a]self-control, and in *your* self-control, [b]perseverance, and in *your* perseverance, [c]godliness, 7 and in *your* godliness, [a]brotherly kindness, and in *your* brotherly kindness, love. 8 For if these *qualities* are yours and are increasing, they render you neither useless nor [a]unfruitful in the true [b]knowledge of our Lord Jesus Christ. 9 For he who lacks these *qualities* is [a]blind *or* short-sighted, having forgotten *his* [b]purification from his former sins. 10

and election sure, by your good actions: for, by so doing, ye will never fall away. 11 For thus will entrance be given you abundantly, into the everlasting kingdom of our Lord and Redeemer Jesus the Messiah. 12 And for this reason I am not wearied in reminding you continually of these things; although ye know them well, and are established in this truth. 13 And it seemeth right to me, so long as I am in this body, to excite you by monition; 14 since I know, that the demise of my body is speedy, as also my Lord Jesus the Messiah hath showed me. 15 And I am anxious, that, after my departure, ye too may have it always with you to make mention of these things. 16 For we have not gone after fables artfully framed, in making known to you the power and advent of our Lord Jesus the Messiah; but [it was] after we had been spectators of his majesty. 17 For, when he received from God the Father honor and glory, and, after the splendid glory of his majesty, a voice came to him thus: This is my beloved Son, in whom I am well pleased; 18 we also heard this identical voice from heaven, which came to him while we were with him in the holy mount. 19 And we have moreover a sure word of prophecy; and ye will do well, if ye look to it as to a light that shineth in a dark place, until the day shall dawn, and the sun shall arise in your hearts; 20 ye having the previous knowledge, that no prophecy is an exposition of its own text. 21 For at no time was it by the pleasure of man, that the prophecy came; but holy men of God spoke, as they were moved by the Holy Spirit.

Therefore, brethren, be all the more diligent to make certain about His *a*calling and *b*choosing you; for as long as you practice these things, you will never *c*stumble; **11** for in this way the entrance into *a*the eternal kingdom of our *b*Lord and Savior Jesus Christ will be *c*abundantly *d*supplied to you.

2Peter 1:12 Therefore, *a*I will always be ready to remind you of these things, even though you *already* know *them,* and have been established in *b*the truth which is present with *you.* **13** I consider it *a*right, as long as I am in *b*this *earthly* dwelling, to *c*stir you up by way of reminder, **14** knowing that *a*the laying aside of my *earthly* dwelling is imminent, *b*as also our Lord Jesus Christ has made clear to me. **15** And I will also be diligent that at any time after my *a*departure you will be able to call these things to mind.

2Peter 1:16 For we did not follow cleverly devised *a*tales when we made known to you the *b*power and coming of our Lord Jesus Christ, but we were *c*eyewitnesses of His majesty. **17** For when He received honor and glory from God the Father, such an [1a]utterance as this was [2]made to Him by the *b*Majestic Glory, "This is My beloved Son with whom I am well-pleased" — **18** and we ourselves heard this [1]utterance made from heaven when we were with Him on the *a*holy mountain.

2Peter 1:19 [1]*So* we have *a*the prophetic word *made* more *b*sure, to which you do well to pay attention as to *c*a lamp shining in a dark place, until the *d*day dawns and

<table>
<tr><td></td><td>the ^emorning star arises ^fin your hearts. **20** But ^aknow this first of all, that ^bno prophecy of Scripture is *a matter* of one's own interpretation, **21** for ^ano prophecy was ever made by an act of human will, but men ^bmoved by the Holy Spirit spoke from God.</td></tr>
</table>

1 Peter 1:1

[a] 2 Pet. 1:1

[b] 1 Pet. 2:11

[c] James. 1:1

[d] Acts. 2:9

[e] Acts. 16:6

[f] Acts. 2:9

[g] Acts. 2:9

[h] Acts. 16:7

[i] Matt. 24:22; Luke 18:7

1 Peter 1:2

[a] Rom. 8:29; 1 Pet. 1:20

[b] 2 Thess. 2:13

[1] Lit *unto obedience and sprinkling*

[c] 1 Pet. 1:14, 22

[d] Heb. 10:22; 12:24

[e] 2 Pet. 1:2

1 Peter 1:3

[a] 2 Cor. 1:3

[b] Gal. 6:16; Titus 3:5

[c] James. 1:18; 1 Pet. 1:23

[d] 1 Pet. 1:13, 21; 3:5, 15; 1 John 3:3

^e 1 Cor. 15:20; 1 Pet. 3:21

1 Peter 1:4

^a Acts. 20:32; Rom. 8:17; Col. 3:24

^b 1 Pet. 5:4

^c 2 Tim. 4:8

1 Peter 1:5

^a John 10:28; Phil. 4:7

^b Eph. 2:8

^c 1 Cor. 1:21; 2 Thess. 2:13

^d 1 Pet. 4:13; 5:1

1 Peter 1:6

^a Rom. 5:2

^b 1 Pet. 5:10

^c 1 Pet. 3:17

^d James. 1:2; 1 Pet. 4:12

¹ Or *temptations*

1 Peter 1:7

¹ Or *genuineness*

^a James. 1:3

^b 1 Cor. 3:13

^c Rom. 2:7

^d Luke 17:30; 1 Pet. 1:13; 4:13

1 Peter 1:8

^a John 20:29

^b Eph. 3:19

¹ Lit *glorified*

1 Peter 1:9

^a Rom. 6:22

¹ One early ms does not contain *your*

1 Peter 1:10

^a Matt. 13:17; Luke 10:24

^b Matt. 26:24

^c 1 Pet. 1:13

1 Peter 1:11

¹ Or *inquiring*

^a 2 Pet. 1:21

^b Matt. 26:24

² Lit *after these*

1 Peter 1:12

^a 1 Pet. 1:25; 4:6

^b Acts. 2:2-4

^c 1 Tim. 3:16

¹ Or *gain a clear glimpse*

1 Peter 1:13

[1] Lit *belt up the waist of your mind*

[a] Eph. 6:14

[2] Lit *be sober*

[b] 1 Thess. 5:6, 8; 2 Tim. 4:5; 1 Pet. 4:7; 5:8

[c] 1 Pet. 1:3

[d] 1 Pet. 1:10

[e] 1 Pet. 1:7

1 Peter 1:14

[1] Lit *children of obedience*

[a] 1 Pet. 1:2

[2] Or *conform yourselves*

[b] Rom. 12:2; 1 Pet. 4:2f

[c] Eph. 4:18

1 Peter 1:15

[1] Lit *according to*

[a] 1 Thess. 4:7; 1 John 3:3

[2] Or *become*

[b] 2 Cor. 7:1

[c] James. 3:13

1 Peter 1:16

[a] Lev 11:44f; 19:2; 20:7

1 Peter 1:17

[a] Ps. 89:26; Jer. 3:19; Matt. 6:9

[b] Acts. 10:34

[c] Matt. 16:27

[d] 2 Cor. 7:1; Heb. 12:28; 1 Pet. 3:15

[e] 1 Pet. 2:11

1 Peter 1:18

[1] Or *ransomed*

[a] Is. 52:3; 1 Cor. 6:20; Titus 2:14; Heb. 9:12

[b] Eph. 4:17

1 Peter 1:19

[a] Acts. 20:28; 1 Pet. 1:2

[b] John 1:29

1 Peter 1:20

[a] Acts. 2:23; Eph. 1:4; 1 Pet. 1:2; Rev. 13:8

[b] Matt. 25:34

[c] Heb. 9:26

[1] Lit *at the end of the times*

[d] Heb. 2:14

1 Peter 1:21

[a] Rom. 4:24; 10:9

[b] John 17:5, 24; 1 Tim. 3:16; Heb. 2:9

[c] 1 Pet. 1:3

1 Peter 1:22

[a] James. 4:8

[b] 1 Pet. 1:2

[c] John 13:34; Rom. 12:10; Heb. 13:1; 1 Pet. 2:17; 3:8

[1] Two early mss *a pure heart*

1 Peter 1:23

[a] John 3:3; 1 Pet. 1:3

[b] John 1:13

[c] Heb. 4:12

1 Peter 1:24

[a] Is 40:6ff; James 1:10f

1 Peter 1:25

[a] Is. 40:8

[b] Heb. 6:5

[1] Lit *preached as good news to you*

Koine Greek

2Peter 1:1   Συμεὼν Πέτρος, δοῦλος καὶ ἀπόστολος Ἰησοῦ χριστοῦ, τοῖς ἰσότιμον ἡμῖν λαχοῦσιν πίστιν ἐν δικαιοσύνῃ τοῦ θεοῦ ἡμῶν καὶ σωτῆρος Ἰησοῦ χριστοῦ· 2 χάρις ὑμῖν καὶ εἰρήνη πληθυνθείη ἐν ἐπιγνώσει τοῦ θεοῦ, καὶ Ἰησοῦ τοῦ κυρίου ἡμῶν· 3 Ὡς πάντα ἡμῖν τῆς θείας δυνάμεως αὐτοῦ τὰ πρὸς ζωὴν καὶ εὐσέβειαν δεδωρημένης, διὰ τῆς ἐπιγνώσεως τοῦ καλέσαντος ἡμᾶς διὰ δόξης καὶ ἀρετῆς· 4 δι' ὦν τὰ τίμια ἡμῖν καὶ μέγιστα ἐπαγγέλματα δεδώρηται, ἵνα διὰ τούτων γένησθε θείας κοινωνοὶ φύσεως, ἀποφυγόντες τῆς ἐν κόσμῳ ἐν ἐπιθυμίᾳ φθορᾶς. 5 Καὶ αὐτὸ τοῦτο δέ, σπουδὴν πᾶσαν παρεισενέγκαντες, ἐπιχορηγήσατε ἐν τῇ πίστει ὑμῶν τὴν ἀρετήν, ἐν δὲ τῇ ἀρετῇ τὴν γνῶσιν, 6 ἐν δὲ τῇ γνώσει τὴν ἐγκράτειαν, ἐν δὲ τῇ ἐγκρατείᾳ τὴν ὑπομονήν, ἐν δὲ τῇ ὑπομονῇ τὴν εὐσέβειαν, 7 ἐν δὲ τῇ εὐσεβείᾳ τὴν φιλαδελφίαν, ἐν δὲ τῇ φιλαδελφίᾳ τὴν ἀγάπην. 8 Ταῦτα γὰρ ὑμῖν ὑπάρχοντα καὶ πλεονάζοντα, οὐκ ἀργοὺς οὐδὲ ἀκάρπους καθίστησιν εἰς τὴν τοῦ κυρίου ἡμῶν Ἰησοῦ χριστοῦ ἐπίγνωσιν. 9 Ὡ γὰρ μὴ πάρεστιν ταῦτα, τυφλός ἐστιν, μυωπάζων, λήθην λαβὼν τοῦ καθαρισμοῦ τῶν πάλαι αὐτοῦ ἁμαρτιῶν. 10 Διὸ μᾶλλον, ἀδελφοί, σπουδάσατε βεβαίαν ὑμῶν τὴν κλῆσιν καὶ ἐκλογὴν ποιεῖσθαι· ταῦτα γὰρ ποιοῦντες οὐ μὴ πταίσητέ ποτε· 11 οὕτως γὰρ πλουσίως ἐπιχορηγηθήσεται ὑμῖν ἡ εἴσοδος εἰς τὴν αἰώνιον βασιλείαν τοῦ κυρίου ἡμῶν καὶ σωτῆρος Ἰησοῦ χριστοῦ.

2Peter 1:12   Διὸ οὐκ ἀμελήσω ἀεὶ ὑμᾶς ὑπομιμνήσκειν περὶ τούτων, καίπερ εἰδότας, καὶ ἐστηριγμένους ἐν τῇ παρούσῃ ἀληθείᾳ. 13 Δίκαιον δὲ ἡγοῦμαι, ἐφ' ὅσον εἰμὶ ἐν τούτῳ τῷ σκηνώματι, διεγείρειν ὑμᾶς ἐν ὑπομνήσει· 14 εἰδὼς ὅτι ταχινή ἐστιν ἡ ἀπόθεσις τοῦ σκηνώματός μου, καθὼς καὶ ὁ κύριος ἡμῶν Ἰησοῦς χριστὸς ἐδήλωσέν μοι. 15 Σπουδάσω δὲ καὶ ἑκάστοτε ἔχειν ὑμᾶς μετὰ τὴν ἐμὴν ἔξοδον τὴν τούτων μνήμην ποιεῖσθαι. 16 Οὐ γὰρ σεσοφισμένοις μύθοις ἐξακολουθήσαντες ἐγνωρίσαμεν ὑμῖν τὴν τοῦ κυρίου ἡμῶν Ἰησοῦ χριστοῦ δύναμιν καὶ παρουσίαν, ἀλλ' ἐπόπται γενηθέντες τῆς ἐκείνου μεγαλειότητος. 17 Λαβὼν γὰρ παρὰ θεοῦ πατρὸς τιμὴν καὶ δόξαν, φωνῆς ἐνεχθείσης αὐτῷ τοιᾶσδε ὑπὸ τῆς μεγαλοπρεποῦς δόξης, Οὗτός ἐστιν ὁ υἱός μου ὁ ἀγαπητός, εἰς ὃν ἐγὼ εὐδόκησα· 18 καὶ ταύτην τὴν φωνὴν ἡμεῖς ἠκούσαμεν ἐξ οὐρανοῦ ἐνεχθεῖσαν, σὺν αὐτῷ ὄντες ἐν τῷ ὄρει τῷ ἁγίῳ. 19 Καὶ ἔχομεν βεβαιότερον τὸν προφητικὸν λόγον, ᾧ καλῶς ποιεῖτε προσέχοντες, ὡς λύχνῳ φαίνοντι ἐν αὐχμηρῷ τόπῳ, ἕως οὗ ἡμέρα διαυγάσῃ, καὶ φωσφόρος ἀνατείλῃ ἐν ταῖς καρδίαις ὑμῶν· 20 τοῦτο πρῶτον γινώσκοντες, ὅτι πᾶσα προφητεία γραφῆς ἰδίας ἐπιλύσεως οὐ γίνεται. 21 Οὐ γὰρ θελήματι ἀνθρώπου ἠνέχθη ποτὲ προφητεία, ἀλλ' ὑπὸ πνεύματος ἁγίου φερόμενοι ἐλάλησαν ἅγιοι θεοῦ ἄνθρωποι.

Language

Process of Discovery

Linguistics Section

Linguistic Structure

[Introduction] 2Peter 1:1   ¹Simon Peter, a *ᵃ*bond-servant and *ᵇ*apostle of Jesus Christ,

A To those who have received *ᶜ*a faith of the same ²kind as ours, ³by *ᵈ*the righteousness of *ᵉ*our God and Savior, Jesus Christ: 2 *ᵃ*Grace and peace be multiplied to you in *ᵇ*the knowledge of God and of Jesus our Lord;

> **B** 3 seeing that His *ᵃ*divine power has granted to us everything pertaining to life and godliness, through the true *ᵇ*knowledge of Him who *ᶜ*called us ¹by His own glory and ²excellence. 4 ¹For by these He has granted to us His precious and magnificent *ᵃ*promises, so that by them you may become *ᵇ*partakers of *the* divine nature, having *ᶜ*escaped the *ᵈ*corruption that is in *ᵉ*the world by lust.

> > **C** 5 Now for this very reason also, applying all diligence, in your faith *ᵃ*supply *ᵇ*moral ¹excellence, and in *your* moral excellence, *ᶜ*knowledge, 6 and in *your* knowledge, *ᵃ*self-control, and in *your* self-control, *ᵇ*perseverance, and in *your* perseverance, *ᶜ*godliness, 7 and in *your* godliness, *ᵃ*brotherly kindness, and in *your* brotherly kindness, love.

> **B'** 8 For if these *qualities* are yours and are increasing, they render you neither useless nor *ᵃ*unfruitful' in the true *ᵇ*knowledge of our Lord Jesus Christ. 9 For he who lacks these *qualities* is *ᵃ*blind *or* short-sighted, having forgotten *his* *ᵇ*purification from his former sins.

A' 10 Therefore, brethren, be all the more diligent to make certain about His *ᵃ*calling and *ᵇ*choosing you; for as long as you practice these things, you will never *ᶜ*stumble; 11 for in this way the entrance into *ᵃ*the eternal kingdom of our *ᵇ*Lord and Savior Jesus Christ will be *ᶜ*abundantly *ᵈ*supplied to you.

A 12 Therefore, *ᵃ*I will always be ready to remind you of these things, even though you *already* know *them,* and have been established in *ᵇ*the truth which is present with *you.* 13 I consider it *ᵃ*right, as long as I am in *ᵇ*this *earthly* dwelling, to *ᶜ*stir you up by way of reminder, 14 knowing that *ᵃ*the laying aside of my *earthly* dwelling is imminent, *ᵇ*as also our Lord Jesus Christ has made clear to me. 15 And I will also be diligent that at any time after my *ᵃ*departure you will be able to call these things to mind.

B 16   For we did not follow cleverly devised [a]tales when we made known to you the [b]power and coming of our Lord Jesus Christ, but we were [c]eyewitnesses of His majesty. 17 For when He received honor and glory from God the Father, such an [1a]utterance as this was [2]made to Him by the [b]Majestic Glory, "This is My beloved Son with whom I am well-pleased" — 18 and we ourselves heard this [1]utterance made from heaven when we were with Him on the [a]holy mountain.

A 19   [1]*So* we have [a]the prophetic word *made* more [b]sure, to which you do well to pay attention as to [c]a lamp shining in a dark place, until the [d]day dawns and the [e]morning star arises [f]in your hearts. 20 But [a]know this first of all, that [b]no prophecy of Scripture is *a matter* of one's own interpretation, 21 for [a]no prophecy was ever made by an act of human will, but men [b]moved by the Holy Spirit spoke from God.

Discussion

More exhortations that seem like a continuation from the previous letter. The problem of people being influenced by alternate Christian experiences was a problem for the Proto-Orthodox church.

Questioning the Passage

1. What does verse one mean?   (explain the formula that a faith in Gods' righteousness…)

   This verse identifies the author of the letter as the apostle Peter, one of Jesus' closest followers. The author emphasizes his role as both a servant of Christ and an apostle, meaning he was sent by Christ to preach the gospel. The author is writing to a specific group of people, those who have received a genuine faith in Yeshua, a faith that is equal in quality to his own. Scholars do not believe that the author is Peter the apostle and they date the letter well after Peter's death. The authorship could have been redacted to a letter from an author who learned about Yeshua through a chain of teachers reaching back to Peter.

"By the righteousness of our God and Savior Jesus Christ" highlights the source of their faith. It was not earned or achieved through their own efforts, but rather received as a gift from God through the righteousness (justice and holiness) of Jesus Christ.

2 Peter 1:1 introduces the letter and its audience. The author is writing to fellow believers who share his faith in Yeshua reminding them of the source and nature of their salvation.

2. Does verse three indicate a divine attribute to Yeshua?

   This verse is future proof that the author was not Peter the Apostle. The idea of Yeshua being God was not introduced until Paul converted the Mithras House churches changing the deity from Mithras to Yeshua of Nazareth. Calling upon a divine power of Yeshua was not an idea in Yeshua's time. The Messianic tradition of that time was that the Messiah was a "special" prophet from the LORD, not God on Earth. The prophets said that when the LORD returned to Earth the day of judgment would occur. Since that did not occur when Yeshua was born the divinity issue during Yeshua's life can be questioned. After the resurrection the spiritual image of Yeshua visited the apostles. At that moment Yeshua could have been granted divine powers by the LORD. This would indicate that the Messiah had been granted divine powers but not that he himself was God.

3. What was Yeshua's glory and moral excellence? (v. 3)

The glory and moral excellence is a reference to the way Yeshua ran his life. He was always concerned about the marginal people in society and did whatever he could to ease their suffering. The glory of Yeshua is usually a reference to the resurrection and ascension. In John's Gospel Yeshua is glorified when he returned to heaven to sit at the right hand of God.

4. What are Yeshua's promises? (v. 4)

- Eternal Life: "For God so loved the world that He gave His only begotten Son, that whoever believes in Him should not perish but have everlasting life).

- Salvation: "He who believes and is baptized shall be saved" (Mark 16:15-16).

- Friendship with God: "You are my friends if you do whatever I command you" (John 15:14).

- Rest and Relief: "Come to me, all you who labor and are heavy laden, and I will give you rest" (Matthew 11:28-30).

- Security in Christ: "The one who comes to me I will certainly not cast out" (John 6:37).

- Eternal Life Assurance: "My sheep listen to My voice; I know them, and they follow Me. I give them eternal life, and they will never perish. No one can snatch them out of My hand" (John 10:27-29).

- Constant Presence: "Lo, I am with you always, even to the end of the age" (Matthew 28:18-20).

- Heavenly Dwelling: "I go to prepare a place for you, and if I go and prepare a place for you, I will come again and receive you to Myself, that where I am, there you may be also" (John 14:1-3).

- Resurrection: "The hour is coming in which all who are in the tombs shall hear the voice of the Son of Man, and they shall come forth—those who have done good, to the resurrection of life, and those who have done evil, to the resurrection of damnation" (John 5:28-29).

- Spiritual Satisfaction: "Whoever drinks of the water that I shall give him shall never thirst again. For the water that I shall give him will become in him a fountain of water springing up into eternal life" (John 4:13-15).

These promises assure us of fellowship with God, victory over death, guidance, and the hope of eternity. Jesus fulfills every promise, securing blessings for believers through His resurrection and the seal of His Spirit upon us.

5. How does one participant in God's divine nature? (v. 4)

The phrase "his divine power" refers to the power of God, which is supernatural and beyond human comprehension.

The phrase "has given us everything we need for life and godliness" means that through faith in Christ, believers have everything they need to live a fulfilling and holy life. This includes spiritual nourishment, strength, guidance, and ultimately, eternal life.

The phrase "through the knowledge of him who called us" emphasizes that this provision comes through knowing and understanding God. The more we learn about God, the more we are equipped to live according to His will.

The phrase "by his own glory and goodness" means God's power and provision are motivated by His own glory (His inherent excellence) and goodness (His loving character).

This verse teaches that God has generously equipped believers with everything they need for a meaningful and holy life through their relationship with Him. It's a reminder that we do not have to struggle alone; God's power is available to us through His Word and His Spirit.

6. What does verse 5, 6 and 7 mean?

The author is urging believers to actively cultivate and grow in their Christian life. Faith is the foundation, but it needs to be built upon other virtues. He lists a series of virtues that should be progressively developed. The list is:

- Goodness: Living a morally upright life, reflecting God's character.
- Knowledge: Growing in understanding of God's Word and His will.
- Self-control: Exercising discipline and restraint in thoughts, words, and actions.
- Perseverance: Enduring through difficulties and remaining faithful to Christ.
- Godliness: Living a life that honors and pleases God.
- Brotherly kindness: Showing love and compassion to other believers.
- Love: The ultimate expression of Christian character, encompassing all the other virtues.

The author emphasizes the practical benefit of these virtues. They equip believers to live a fruitful and meaningful life, demonstrating the reality of their faith.

These three verses encourages believers to move beyond a passive faith and actively cultivate a life marked by increasing godliness and love.

7. What is the true knowledge of Yeshua? (v. 8)
The author is making a reference to the proto-Orthodox church beliefs and doctrines. During the first century of Christianity there were at least five major expressions of what Yeshua's life and message was about. Naturally, the proto-Orthodox Church believe that it was the only keeper of the true knowledge.

8. What action does a "follower" need to show to be a true follower, thus knowing the knowledge? (v. 8)
A follower needs to do the following things, which was listed in the previous verses, faith, virtue, knowledge, self-control, perseverance, godliness, brotherly kindness, and love.

9. How are sins cleansed? (v. 9)
The Christian Bible teaches that our sins are forgiven and cleansed through the sacrifice of Yeshua on the cross. He took the punishment for our sins, so that we could be reconciled to God. To receive this forgiveness, we must repent of our sins (turn away from them) and place our faith in Yeshua as our Lord and Savior. The Holy Spirit helps us to live a life that is pleasing to God and to resist temptation. He also empowers us to confess our sins and receive forgiveness. (

In essence, our sins are cleansed through God's grace, received through faith in Yeshua the Messiah and empowered by the Holy Spirit.

10. What is the process of election into the faith? (v. 10)

in this verse the author is referring to God's plan for one's life and one's chosen place in God's family. It is about solidifying your commitment to following Yeshua was ways.

11. How does the author know he is about to die? (v. 14)

it was a reality at the time of the writing of this letter that Christian leaders were being tortured, put in prison and killed. By the author writing this letter the authorities would know enough about him to grab him and arrest him.

12. Why the noun change to "we" from "I?" (v. 15)

In 2 Peter, the pronoun usage changes from "I" to "we" in verse 15. This is a common literary technique used by ancient writers, and there are a few possible reasons why Peter might have done this:By using "we," Peter might be trying to create a sense of unity and shared experience with his readers. He's not just speaking as an individual, but as part of a larger community of believers.

The use of "we" could also be a way of emphasizing the apostolic authority of the letter. Peter is writing not just as himself, but as a representative of the apostles and the early church.

The shift from "I" to "we" might also mark a transition in the letter's focus. After introducing himself in verse 15, Peter moves on to address broader themes and concerns of the Christian community.

It's important to remember that without more context, it's difficult to say for sure what Peter's exact intention was.

13. Does verse sixteen give proof to the author being Peter Simon? (v. 16)
this verse insinuates that the author was one of the original disciples. This is in conflict with scholars who believe this letter was written after 100 CE. It is possible that the letter was redacted over time, especially when the church decided it was a Peter letter, to reflect some authority in the letter since it was being placed inside of the New Testament Bible.

14. What is honor and glory in verse seventeen?
The author is directly addressing any potential doubts about the truthfulness of his message. He's saying that he and the other apostles weren't spreading fabricated stories or empty legends.

The power of Yeshua is the core message of the Christian faith for the proto-orthodox church: Jesus's resurrection, his power over death, and his return in glory.

The author is emphasizing that he and the other apostles personally witnessed the resurrected Yeshua. They saw his glory and power firsthand. This is in contradiction to the idea that the letter was penned after 100 CE. However, it is hard to believe that the ideas that have been expressed in the first letter and this one were developed by Peter only a decade or so after Yeshua was resurrection.

The author is saying that the Christian message is not based on hearsay or imagination. It's grounded in the real, historical experience of seeing Jesus alive after his death. He and the other apostles weren't just repeating stories; they were sharing what they had personally seen and experienced. The interpretation of the meaning of Yeshua's life and death was in several different ways during the beginning centuries of Christianity. It is difficult to know who had the correct interpretation. However, the proto-Orthodox church, which came from Paul's conversion of the Mithras churches, became the dominant force of Christianity and that was the religion that was adopted by Constantine in 325 CE.

15. What is Majestic Glory? (v. 17)

The author is referring to the resurrection of Yeshua and his appearance to the women in his disciples.

16. What mountain is referred to in verse eighteen?

The name of the mountain is not mentioned in this verse. However, it could simply be a reference that several God miracles occurred on mountaintops. For example, on Mount Sinai Moses received the 10 Commandments and the Torah from God. On Mount Tabor the prophets of the baal. Jerusalem and the Temple sat on the top of Mount Zion. The transfiguration occurred on a mountain top. Therefore, mountains appear to be considered high and holy places.

17. What is the morning star? (v. 19)

The morning star has long been a symbol of hope, light, and new beginnings. It appears just before the sun rises, bringing the promise of a new day.

Throughout the Christian Bible, Yeshua is often referred to as the "light of the world." He brings truth, guidance, and salvation to humanity.

The author is saying that the prophecies Yeshua have been fulfilled in him, and his coming is a sure and certain hope. Just as the morning star brings light to a dark world, Yeshua brings light and hope to our lives.

Thoughts

This chapter has several exhortations for the people to follow.

1 Peter Chapter Two

Language

Peshitta	New American Standard 1995
2Peter 2:1 But in the world, there have been also false prophets, as there will likewise be false teachers among you, who will bring in destructive heresies, denying the Lord that bought them; thus bringing on themselves swift destruction. 2 And many will go after their profaneness; on account of whom, the way of truth will be reproached. 3 And, in the cupidity of raving words, they will make merchandise of you: whose judgment, of a long time, is not idle; and their destruction slumbereth not. 4 For, if God spared not the angels that sinned, but cast them down to the infernal regions in chains of darkness, and delivered them up to be kept unto the judgment of torture, 5 and spared not the former world, but preserved Noah the eighth person, a preacher of righteousness, when he brought a flood on the world of the wicked; 6 [and] burned up the cities of Sodom and Gomorrah, and condemned them by an overthrow, making them a demonstration to the wicked who should come after them; 7 and also delivered righteous Lot, who was tormented with the filthy conduct of the lawless; 8 for that upright man dwelling among them, in seeing and hearing from day to day, was distressed in his righteous soul by their lawless deeds; 9 the Lord knoweth how to rescue from afflictions those who fear him; and he will reserve the wicked for the day of judgment to be tormented, 10 and	2Peter 2:1 But *a*false prophets also arose among the people, just as there will also be *b*false teachers *c*among you, who will *d*secretly introduce *e*destructive heresies, even *f*denying the *g*Master who *h*bought them, bringing swift destruction upon themselves. 2 Many will follow their *a*sensuality, and because of them *b*the way of the truth will be *c*maligned; 3 and in *their* *a*greed they will *b*exploit you with *c*false words; *d*their judgment from long ago is not idle, and their destruction is not asleep. 2Peter 2:4 For *a*if God did not spare angels when they sinned, but cast them into hell and *b*committed them to pits of darkness, reserved for judgment; 5 and did not spare *a*the ancient world, but preserved *b*Noah, a *1*preacher of righteousness, with seven others, when He brought a *c*flood upon the world of the ungodly; 6 and *if* He *a*condemned the cities of Sodom and Gomorrah to destruction by reducing *them* to ashes, having made them an *b*example to those who would *1*live ungodly *lives* thereafter; 7 and *if* He *a*rescued righteous Lot, oppressed by the *b*sensual conduct of *c*unprincipled men 8 (for by what he saw and heard *that* *a*righteous man, while living among them, felt *his* righteous soul tormented day after day by *their* lawless deeds), 9 *a*then the Lord knows how to rescue the godly from *1*temptation, and to keep the unrighteous under punishment

especially them who go after the flesh in the lusts of pollution, and despise government. Daring and arrogant, they shudder not with awe while they blaspheme; 11 whereas angels, greater than they in might and valor, bring not against them a reproachful denunciation. 12 But these, like the dumb beasts that by nature are for slaughter and corruption, while reviling the things they know not, will perish in their own corruption; 13 they being persons with whom iniquity is the reward of iniquity, and by them rioting in the daytime is accounted delightful; defiled and full of spots [are they], indulging themselves at their ease, while they give themselves up to pleasure; 14 having eyes that are full of adultery, and sins that never end; seducing unstable souls; and having a heart exercised in cupidity; children of malediction: 15 and, having left the way of rectitude, they have wandered and gone in the way of Balaam the son of Beor, who loved the wages of iniquity, 16 and who had for the reprover of his transgression a dumb ass, which, speaking with the speech of men, rebuked the madness of the prophet. 17 These are wells without water, clouds driven by a tempest, persons for whom is reserved the blackness of darkness. 18 For, while they utter astonishing vanity, they seduce, with obscene lusts of the flesh, them who have almost abandoned these that walk in error. 19 And they promise them liberty, while they themselves are the slaves of corruption: for, by whatever thing a man is vanquished, to that is he enslaved. 20 For if, when they have escaped the pollutions of the world by the knowledge of our Lord and Redeemer Jesus the

for the [b]day of judgment, 10 and especially those who [1a]indulge the flesh in *its* corrupt desires and [b]despise authority.

Daring, [c]self-willed, they do not tremble when they [b]revile angelic [2]majesties, 11 [a]whereas angels who are greater in might and power do not bring a reviling judgment against them before the Lord. 12 But [a]these, like unreasoning animals, [b]born as creatures of instinct to be captured and killed, reviling where they have no knowledge, will in [1]the destruction of those creatures also be destroyed, 13 suffering wrong as [a]the wages of doing wrong. They count it a pleasure to [b]revel in the [c]daytime. They are stains and blemishes, [b]reveling in their [1]deceptions, as they [d]carouse with you, 14 having eyes full of adultery that never cease from sin, [a]enticing [b]unstable souls, having a heart trained in [c]greed, [d]accursed children; 15 forsaking [a]the right way, they have gone astray, having followed [b]the way of Balaam, the *son* of Beor, who loved [c]the wages of unrighteousness; 16 but he received a rebuke for his own transgression, [a]*for* a mute donkey, speaking with a voice of a man, restrained the madness of the prophet.

2Peter 2:17 These are [a]springs without water and mists driven by a storm, [b]for whom the [1]black darkness has been reserved. 18 For speaking out [a]arrogant *words* of [b]vanity they [c]entice by fleshly desires, by [d]sensuality, those who barely [e]escape from the ones who live in error, 19 promising them freedom while they themselves are slaves of corruption; for [a]by what a man is overcome, by this he is

Messiah, they become again involved in the same, and are vanquished, their latter state is worse than the former. 21 For it would have been better for them, not to have known the way of righteousness, than after having known [it], to turn back from the holy commandment that was delivered to them. 22 But the true proverb hath happened to them: the dog returneth to his vomit and the sow that was washed, to her wallowing in the mire.

enslaved. 20 For if, after they have [a]escaped the defilements of the world by [b]the knowledge of the [c]Lord and Savior Jesus Christ, they are again [d]entangled in them and are overcome, [e]the last state has become worse for them than the first. 21 [f]For it would be better for them not to have known the way of righteousness, than having known it, to turn away from [b]the holy commandment [h]handed on to them. 22 [i]It has happened to them according to the true proverb, "[a]A DOG RETURNS TO ITS OWN VOMIT," and, "A sow, after washing, *returns* to wallowing in the mire."

2Peter 2:1
*a*Deut 13:1ff; Jer 6:13
*b*2 Cor 11:13
*c*Matt 7:15; 1 Tim 4:1
*d*Gal 2:4; Jude 4
*e*1 Cor 11:19; Gal 5:20
*f*Jude 4
*g*Rev 6:10
*h*1 Cor 6:20

2Peter 2:2
*a*Gen 19:5ff; 2 Pet 2:7, 18; Jude 4
*b*Acts 16:17; 22:4; 24:14
*c*Rom 2:24

2Peter 2:3
*a*1 Tim 6:5; 2 Pet 2:14; Jude 16
*b*2 Cor 2:17; 1 Thess 2:5
*c*Rom 16:18; 2 Pet 1:16
*d*Deut 32:35

2Peter 2:4
*a*Jude 6
*b*Rev 20:1f2Peter 2:5
[1]Or *herald*
*a*Ezek 26:20; 2 Pet 3:6
*b*Gen 6:8, 9; 1 Pet 3:20
*c*2 Pet 3:6

2Peter 2:6
*a*Gen 19:24; Jude 7
*b*Is 1:9; Matt 10:15; 11:23; Rom 9:29; Jude 7
*c*Jude 15

2Peter 2:7
*a*Gen 19:16, 29
*b*Gen 19:5ff; 2 Pet 2:2, 18; Jude 4

[c]2 Pet 3:17

2Peter 2:8
[a]Heb 11:4

2Peter 2:9
[1]Lit *trial;* or *temptation*
[a]1 Cor 10:13; Rev 3:10
[b]Matt 10:15; Jude 6

2Peter 2:10
[1]Lit *go after*
[2]Lit *glories*
[a]2 Pet 3:3; Jude 16, 18
[b]Ex 22:28; Jude 8
[c]Titus 1:7

2Peter 2:11
[a]Jude 9

2Peter 2:12
[1]Lit *their destruction also*
[a]Jude 10
[b]Jer 12:3; Col 2:22

2Peter 2:13
[1]One early ms reads *love feasts*
[a]2 Pet 2:15
[b]Rom 13:13
[c]1 Thess 5:7
[d]1 Cor 11:21; Jude 12

2Peter 2:14
[a]2 Pet 2:18
[b]James 1:8; 2 Pet 3:16
[c]2 Pet 2:3
[d]Eph 2:3

2Peter 2:15
[a]Acts 13:10
[b]Num 22:5, 7; Deut 23:4; Neh 13:2; Jude 11; Rev 2:14

^e2 Pet 2:13

2Peter 2:16
^aNum 22:21, 23, 28, 30ff

2Peter 2:17
¹Lit *blackness of darkness*
^aJude 12
^bJude 13

2Peter 2:18
^aJude 16
^bEph 4:17
^c2 Pet 2:14
^d2 Pet 2:2
^e2 Pet 1:4; 2:20

2Peter 2:19
^aJohn 8:34; Rom 6:16

2Peter 2:20
^a2 Pet 2:18
^b2 Pet 1:2
^c2 Pet 1:11; 3:18
^d2 Tim 2:4
^eMatt 12:45; Luke 11:26

2Peter 2:21
^aEzek 18:24; Heb 6:4ff; 10:26f; James 4:17
^bGal 6:2; 1 Tim 6:14; 2 Pet 3:2
^cJude 3

2Peter 2:22
¹Lit *The thing of the true proverb has happened to them*
^aProv 26:11

Koine Greek

2Peter 2:1   Ἐγένοντο δὲ καὶ ψευδοπροφῆται ἐν τῷ λαῷ, ὡς καὶ ἐν ὑμῖν ἔσονται ψευδοδιδάσκαλοι, οἵτινες παρεισάξουσιν αἱρέσεις ἀπωλείας, καὶ τὸν ἀγοράσαντα αὐτοὺς δεσπότην ἀρνούμενοι, ἐπάγοντες ἑαυτοῖς ταχινὴν ἀπώλειαν. 2 Καὶ πολλοὶ ἐξακολουθήσουσιν αὐτῶν ταῖς ἀσελγείαις, δι᾽ οὓς ἡ ὁδὸς τῆς ἀληθείας βλασφημηθήσεται. 3 Καὶ ἐν πλεονεξίᾳ πλαστοῖς λόγοις ὑμᾶς ἐμπορεύσονται· οἷς τὸ κρίμα ἔκπαλαι οὐκ ἀργεῖ, καὶ ἡ ἀπώλεια αὐτῶν οὐ νυστάξει. 4 Εἰ γὰρ ὁ θεὸς ἀγγέλων ἁμαρτησάντων οὐκ ἐφείσατο, ἀλλὰ σειραῖς ζόφου ταρταρώσας παρέδωκεν εἰς κρίσιν τηρημένους· 5 καὶ ἀρχαίου κόσμου οὐκ ἐφείσατο, ˊ ἀλλὰ ˋ ὄγδοον Νῶε δικαιοσύνης κήρυκα ἐφύλαξεν, κατακλυσμὸν κόσμῳ ἀσεβῶν ἐπάξας· 6 καὶ πόλεις Σοδόμων καὶ Γομόρρας τεφρώσας καταστροφῇ κατέκρινεν, ὑπόδειγμα μελλόντων ἀσεβεῖν τεθεικώς· 7 καὶ δίκαιον Λῶτ, καταπονούμενον ὑπὸ τῆς τῶν ἀθέσμων ἐν ἀσελγείᾳ ἀναστροφῆς· ἐρρύσατο 8 βλέμματι γὰρ καὶ ἀκοῇ ὁ δίκαιος, ἐγκατοικῶν ἐν αὐτοῖς, ἡμέραν ἐξ ἡμέρας ψυχὴν δικαίαν ἀνόμοις ἔργοις ἐβασάνιζεν· 9 οἶδεν κύριος εὐσεβεῖς ἐκ πειρασμοῦ ῥύεσθαι, ἀδίκους δὲ εἰς ἡμέραν κρίσεως κολαζομένους τηρεῖν· 10 μάλιστα δὲ τοὺς ὀπίσω σαρκὸς ἐν ἐπιθυμίᾳ μιασμοῦ πορευομένους, καὶ κυριότητος καταφρονοῦντας. Τολμηταί, αὐθάδεις, δόξας οὐ τρέμουσιν βλασφημοῦντες· 11 ὅπου ἄγγελοι, ἰσχύϊ καὶ δυνάμει μείζονες ὄντες, οὐ φέρουσιν κατ᾽ αὐτῶν παρὰ κυρίῳ βλάσφημον κρίσιν. 12 Οὗτοι δέ, ὡς ἄλογα ζῷα φυσικὰ γεγενημένα εἰς ἅλωσιν καὶ φθοράν, ἐν οἷς ἀγνοοῦσι βλασφημοῦντες, ἐν τῇ φθορᾷ αὐτῶν καταφθαρήσονται, 13 κομιούμενοι μισθὸν ἀδικίας, ἡδονὴν ἡγούμενοι τὴν ἐν ἡμέρᾳ τρυφήν, σπίλοι καὶ μῶμοι, ἐντρυφῶντες ἐν ταῖς ἀπάταις αὐτῶν συνευωχούμενοι ὑμῖν, 14 ὀφθαλμοὺς ἔχοντες μεστοὺς μοιχαλίδος καὶ ἀκαταπαύστους ἁμαρτίας, δελεάζοντες ψυχὰς ἀστηρίκτους, καρδίαν γεγυμνασμένην πλεονεξίας ἔχοντες, κατάρας τέκνα· 15 καταλιπόντες εὐθεῖαν ὁδὸν ἐπλανήθησαν, ἐξακολουθήσαντες τῇ ὁδῷ τοῦ Βαλαὰμ τοῦ Βοσόρ, ὃς μισθὸν ἀδικίας ἠγάπησεν, 16 ἔλεγξιν δὲ ἔσχεν ἰδίας παρανομίας· ὑποζύγιον ἄφωνον, ἐν ἀνθρώπου φωνῇ φθεγξάμενον, ἐκώλυσεν τὴν τοῦ προφήτου παραφρονίαν. 17 Οὗτοί εἰσιν πηγαὶ ἄνυδροι, νεφέλαι ὑπὸ λαίλαπος ἐλαυνόμεναι, οἷς ὁ ζόφος τοῦ σκότους εἰς αἰῶνα τετήρηται. 18 Ὑπέρογκα γὰρ ματαιότητος φθεγγόμενοι, δελεάζουσιν ἐν ἐπιθυμίαις σαρκός, ἀσελγείαις, τοὺς ὄντως ἀποφυγόντας τοὺς ἐν πλάνῃ ἀναστρεφομένους, 19 ἐλευθερίαν αὐτοῖς ἐπαγγελλόμενοι, αὐτοὶ δοῦλοι ὑπάρχοντες τῆς φθορᾶς· ᾧ γάρ τις ἥττηται, τούτῳ καὶ δεδούλωται. 20 Εἰ γὰρ ἀποφυγόντες τὰ μιάσματα τοῦ κόσμου ἐν ἐπιγνώσει τοῦ κυρίου καὶ σωτῆρος Ἰησοῦ χριστοῦ, τούτοις δὲ πάλιν ἐμπλακέντες ἡττῶνται, γέγονεν αὐτοῖς τὰ ἔσχατα χείρονα τῶν πρώτων. 21 Κρεῖττον γὰρ ἦν αὐτοῖς μὴ ἐπεγνωκέναι τὴν ὁδὸν τῆς δικαιοσύνης, ἢ ἐπιγνοῦσιν ἐπιστρέψαι ἐκ τῆς παραδοθείσης αὐτοῖς ἁγίας ἐντολῆς. 22 Συμβέβηκεν δὲ αὐτοῖς τὸ τῆς ἀληθοῦς παροιμίας, Κύων ἐπιστρέψας ἐπὶ τὸ ἴδιον ἐξέραμα, καὶ ὗς λουσαμένη εἰς κύλισμα βορβόρου.

Language

  Process of Discovery

   Linguistics Section

    Linguistic Structure

A 1   But *a*false prophets also arose among the people, just as there will also be *b*false teachers *c*among you, who will *d*secretly introduce *e*destructive heresies, even *f*denying the *g*Master who *h*bought them, bringing swift destruction upon themselves. 2 Many will follow their *a*sensuality, and because of them *b*the way of the truth will be *c*maligned; 3 and in *their* *a*greed they will *b*exploit you with *c*false words; *d*their judgment from long ago is not idle, and their destruction is not asleep.

   B 4   For *a*if God did not spare angels when they sinned, but cast them into hell and *b*committed them to pits of darkness, reserved for judgment;

      C 5 and did not spare *a*the ancient world, but preserved *b*Noah, a [1]preacher of righteousness, with seven others, when He brought a *c*flood upon the world of the ungodly;

         D 6 and *if* He *a*condemned the cities of Sodom and Gomorrah to destruction by reducing *them* to ashes, having made them an *b*example to those who would *live ungodly *lives* thereafter;

      C' 7 and *if* He *a*rescued righteous Lot, oppressed by the *b*sensual conduct of *c*unprincipled men 8 (for by what he saw and heard *that* *a*righteous man, while living among them, felt *his* righteous soul tormented day after day by *their* lawless deeds),

   B' 9 *a*then the Lord knows how to rescue the godly from [1]temptation, and to keep the unrighteous under punishment for the *b*day of judgment,

A' 10 and especially those who [1]*a*indulge the flesh in *its* corrupt desires and *b*despise authority. Daring, *c*self-willed, they do not tremble when they *b*revile angelic [2]majesties, 11 *a*whereas angels who are greater in might and power do not bring a reviling judgment against them before the Lord. 12 But *a*these, like unreasoning animals, *b*born as creatures of instinct to be captured and killed, reviling where they have no knowledge, will in [1]the destruction of those creatures also be destroyed,

A 13 suffering wrong as *the wages of doing wrong. They count it a pleasure to *revel in the *daytime. They are stains and blemishes, *reveling in their [1]deceptions, as they *carouse with you, 14 having eyes full of adultery that never cease from sin, *enticing *unstable souls, having a heart trained in *greed, *accursed children; 15 forsaking *the right way, they have gone astray, having followed *the way of Balaam, the *son* of Beor, who loved *the wages of unrighteousness; 16 but he received a rebuke for his own transgression, *for* a mute donkey, speaking with a voice of a man, restrained the madness of the prophet.

> **B** 17 These are *springs without water and mists driven by a storm, *for whom the [1]black darkness has been reserved. 18 For speaking out *arrogant *words* of *vanity they *entice by fleshly desires, by *sensuality, those who barely *escape from the ones who live in error,

A' 19 promising them freedom while they themselves are slaves of corruption; for *by what a man is overcome, by this he is enslaved. 20 For if, after they have *escaped the defilements of the world by *the knowledge of the *Lord and Savior Jesus Christ, they are again *entangled in them and are overcome, *the last state has become worse for them than the first. 21 *For it would be better for them not to have known the way of righteousness, than having known it, to turn away from *the holy commandment *handed on to them. 22 [1]It has happened to them according to the true proverb, "*A DOG RETURNS TO ITS OWN VOMIT," and, "A sow, after washing, *returns* to wallowing in the mire."

Discussion

The protection of Paul's theology was very important to the early church and can

be seen in this chapter. The concerns about false prophets and teachers is clear.

Questioning the Passage

1. Who are the false prophets? (v. 1)

   The false prophets are the other expressions of Christianity that existed in the

   first and second century CE. This letter mimics Paul's letters warning the proto-

   Orthodox churches, which he converted from Mithras house churches that any other understanding of the work of Yeshua was unacceptable. Only Paul's way was accepted. The churches that were receiving these letters were also proto-Orthodox churches.

2. Who is the Master who bought people? (v. 1)

The master in this case is Yeshua.

3. What is the swift destruction? (v. 1)

The swift destruction came from the heresies that were brought by false teachers. The false teachers or anyone who did not express the Pauline view of what Yeshua was all about.

4. How does sensuality destroy truth? (v. 2)

Sensuality often leads to a disregard for moral boundaries and a willingness to compromise with sin. This can manifest by embracing false teachings that justify or minimize immoral behavior.

5. What was the judgment from long ago? (v. 3)

False teachers are already under God's judgment. Their actions and teachings are inherently wrong, and they are facing the consequences of their choices. The judgment on them has already been determined.

6. Who were the sinful angels? (v. 4)

This is a reference to the angels that was described in Genesis 6:1 – six. In Genesis, they were called the Watchers. The full explanation of what happened with the watchers can be found in 1 Enoch.

7. Who were the seven in verse five?

   Noah's wife, three sons, and three daughters-in-law.

8. Is verse five saying that the Flood did not remove all evil, or that humanity is naturally evil? (v. 5 & 6)

   Yes. 199 of the 200 watchers were condemned into the foundations of the earth, according to 1 Enoch. During Yeshua's time, these condemned angels tried to escape by possessing people. Whenever Yeshua did an exorcism, he returned the condemned Watchers back into the foundations of the earth.

9. What does the verses seven through eleven tell us?

   This passage is discussing the judgment of God and the fate of the wicked. The passage emphasizes that God is just and will punish those who do evil. It describes the wicked as being destroyed and suffering eternal punishment. It contrasts the fate of the wicked with the safety and protection of those who are righteous.

10. What does the verses twelve through sixteen?

    These verses refer to false teachers. The passage identifies these individuals as dangerous and deceptive. They are not genuine followers of Christ, but exploit people for their own gain. They are described as being driven by greed, corruption, and a desire for power. They lack true understanding and twist the truth to suit their purposes. They use false teachings and promises of freedom to lure people into their trap. They prey on the vulnerable and innocent.

11. What is a spring without water? (v. 17)

In the near East it was normal during the dry season for a spring or a well to dry up and then it would be abandoned until the rainy season came. Such changes could be so sudden that travelers and shepherds may have come to a well or stream on one day and come back the next day to find that the stream of the well was empty and possibly polluted. The author is equating false teachers to these dry abandoned wells. False teachers are like dry wells full of filth and corruption.

12. What is black darkness? (v. 17)

The black darkness refers to the followers of Yeshua, who are tempted away from the proto-orthodox church to any other expression of Christianity.

13. How can the people be condemned for not being able to think rationally? (v. 17 with reference back to verse 12)

This idea stems from the belief that people who came to know Yeshua as Lord and Savior through the proto-orthodox church will be condemned for believing the false teachers. These false teachers are from all the other Christian expressions that existed in the first 300 years of Christianity. The proto-orthodox church won the day when Constantine made it the religion of the Empire. All other expressions of Christianity were erase from history.

14. Is verse eighteen referring to persons who had recently converted to Christianity?

This verse is referring to people who had left any expression of Christianity other than the proto-orthodox version. These people discovered errors in their ways. The proto-orthodox church was very careful to ensure that their members only heard the "single" interpretation of Yeshua's life. This was the Pauline expression and interpretation of the way things should be.

15. Why did new Christians revert to their previous ways? (v. 20)

The proto-Orthodox church had a problem with people leaving the faith. It was very difficult to live in the Roman Empire and be a part of the proto-Orthodox church. History tells us that there were many people who quit being members of said church and return to their old pagan ways. For example, if a person who had a government job became a Christian of any expression, they immediately lost their job. This would create a tremendous burden because no one would hire that person.

Verse Comparison of citations or proof text

1. 22 [1]It has happened to them according to the true proverb, ""A DOG RETURNS TO ITS OWN VOMIT," and, "A sow, after washing, *returns* to wallowing in the mire."

   Proverbs 26:11 Like [a]a dog that returns to its vomit, So is a fool who [b]repeats [1]his foolishness.

   If one knows their situation is poor and gets out of that situation why would they return to the original situation? It was meant for people who joined the proto-orthodox church then decided to leave it.

Thoughts

The main concern of the author is that people must not leave the proto-Orthodox church once they become a part of it.

Language

Peshitta	New American Standard 2020
2Peter 3:1 This second epistle, my beloved, I now write to you; in [both of] which I stir up your honest mind by admonition: 2 that ye may be mindful of the words which were formerly spoken by the holy prophets, and of the injunction of our Lord and Redeemer by the hand of the legates: 3 knowing this previously, that there will come in the last days scoffers, who will scoff, walking according to their own lusts; 4 and saying, Where is the promise of his coming? for, since our fathers fell asleep, every thing remaineth just as from the beginning of the creation. 5 For this they willingly forget, that the heavens were of old; and the earth rose up from the waters, and by means of water, by the word of God. 6 [And], by means of these [waters], the world which then was, [being submerged] again perished in the waters. 7 And the heavens that now are, and the earth, are by his word stored up, being reserved for the fire at the day of judgment and the perdition of wicked men. 8 And of this one thing, my beloved, be not forgetful, That one day, to the Lord, is as a thousand years; and a thousand years, as one day. 9 The Lord doth not procrastinate his promises, as some estimate procrastination; but he is long suffering, for your sakes, being not willing that any should perish, but that every one should come to repentance. 10 And the day of the Lord will come, like a	2Peter 3:1 [a]Beloved, this is now the second letter I am writing to you in which I am [b]stirring up your sincere mind by way of a reminder, 2 to [a]remember the words spoken beforehand by [b]the holy prophets and [c]the commandment of the Lord and Savior *spoken* by your apostles. 3 [a]Know this first *of all,* that [b]in the last days [c]mockers will come with *their* mocking, [d]following after their own lusts, 4 and saying, "[a]Where is the promise of His [b]coming? For *ever* since the fathers [1c]fell asleep, all things continue just as *they were* [d]from the beginning of creation." 5 For [1]when they maintain this, it escapes their notice that [a]by the word of God *the* heavens existed long ago and *the* earth was [b]formed out of water and by water, 6 through which [a]the world at that time was [b]destroyed by being flooded with water. 7 But by His word [a]the present heavens and earth are being reserved for [b]fire, kept for [c]the day of judgment and destruction of ungodly people. 2Peter 3:8 But do not let this one *fact* escape your notice, [a]beloved, that with the Lord one day is like a thousand years, and [b]a thousand years like one day. 9 [a]The Lord is not slow about His promise, as some count slowness, but [b]is patient toward you, [c]not willing for any to perish, but for all to come to repentance.

thief; in which the heavens will suddenly pass away; and the elements, being ignited, will be dissolved; and the earth and the works in it, will not be found. 11 As therefore all these things are to be dissolved, what persons ought ye to be, in holy conduct, and in the fear of God, 12 expecting and desiring the coming of the day of God, in which the heavens being tried by fire will be dissolved, and the elements being ignited will melt? 13 But we, according to his promise, expect new heavens, and a new earth, in which righteousness dwelleth. 14 Therefore, my beloved, as ye expect these things, strive that ye may be found by him in peace, without spot and without blemish. 15 And account the long suffering of the Lord to be redemption; as also our beloved brother Paul, according to the wisdom conferred on him, wrote to you; 16 as also in all his epistles, speaking in them of these things, in which there is something difficult to be understood; [and] which they who are ignorant and unstable, pervert, as they do also the rest of the scriptures, to their own destruction. 17 Ye therefore, my beloved, as ye know [these things] beforehand, guard yourselves, lest, by going after the error of the lawless, ye fall from your steadfastness. 18 But be ye growing in grace, and in the knowledge of our Lord and Redeemer Jesus the Messiah, and of God the Father: whose is the glory, now, and always, and to the days of eternity. Amen.

10 But [a]the day of the Lord [b]will come like a thief, in which [c]the heavens [d]will pass away with a roar and the [e]elements will be destroyed with intense heat, and [f]the earth and [1]its works will be [2]discovered.

2Peter 3:11   Since all these things are to be destroyed in this way, what sort of people ought you to be in holy conduct and godliness, 12 [a]looking for and hastening the coming of the day of God, because of which [b]the heavens will be destroyed by burning, and the [c]elements will melt with intense heat! 13 But according to His [a]promise we are looking for [b]new heavens and a new earth, [c]in which righteousness dwells.

2Peter 3:14   [a]Therefore, [b]beloved, since you look for these things, be diligent to be [c]found [d]spotless and blameless by Him, at peace, 15 and regard the [a]patience of our Lord *as* salvation; just as also [b]our beloved brother Paul, [c]according to the wisdom given him, wrote to you, 16 as also in all *his* letters, speaking in them of [a]these things, [b]in which there are some things that are hard to understand, which the untaught and [c]unstable distort, as *they do* also [d]the rest of the Scriptures, to their own destruction. 17 You therefore, [a]beloved, knowing this beforehand, [b]be on your guard so that you are not carried away by [c]the error of [1d]unscrupulous people and [e]lose your own [2]firm commitment, 18 but grow in the grace and [a]knowledge of our [b]Lord and Savior Jesus Christ. [c]To Him *be* the glory, both now and to the day of eternity. Amen.

2 Peter 3:1
[a] 1 Pet. 2:11; 2 Pet. 3:8, 14, 17
[b] 2 Pet. 1:13

2 Peter 3:2
[a] Jude 17
[b] Luke 1:70; Acts. 3:21; Eph. 3:5
[c] Gal. 6:2; 1 Tim. 6:14; 2 Pet. 2:21

The Coming Day of the Lord (2 Peter 3:3-3:9)

2 Peter 3:3
[a] 2 Pet. 1:20
[b] 1 Tim. 4:1; Heb. 1:2
[c] Jude 18
[d] 2 Pet. 2:10

2 Peter 3:4
[a] Is. 5:19; Jer. 17:15; Ezek. 11:3; 12:22, 27; Mal. 2:17; Matt. 24:48
[b] 1 Thess. 2:19; 2 Pet. 3:12
[1] I.e., died
[c] Acts. 7:60
[d] Mark 10:6

2 Peter 3:5
[1] Or *they are willfully ignorant of this fact, that*
[a] Gen. 1:6, 9; Heb. 11:3
[b] Ps. 24:2; 136:6

2 Peter 3:6
[a] 2 Pet. 2:5
[b] Gen. 7:11, 12, 21f

2 Peter 3:7
[a] 2 Pet. 3:10, 12
[b] Is. 66:15; Dan 7:9f; 2 Thess. 1:7; Heb. 12:29

^c Matt. 10:15; 1 Cor. 3:13; Jude 7

2 Peter 3:8
^a 2 Pet. 3:1
^b Ps. 90:4

2 Peter 3:9
^a Hab. 2:3; Rom. 13:11; Heb. 10:37
^b Rom. 2:4; Rev. 2:21
^c 1 Tim. 2:4; Rev. 2:21

A New Heaven and Earth (2 Peter 3:10-3:18)

2 Peter 3:10
^a 1 Cor. 1:8
^b Matt. 24:43; Luke 12:39; 1 Thess. 5:2; Rev. 3:3; 16:15
^c Is. 34:4; 2 Pet. 3:7, 12
^d Matt. 24:35; Rev. 21:1
^e Is. 24:19; Mic. 1:4
^f 2 Pet. 3:7
[1] Lit *the works in it*
[2] I.e., as worthless; late mss *burned up*

2 Peter 3:12
^a 1 Cor. 1:7
^b 2 Pet. 3:7, 10
^c Is. 24:19; 34:4; Mic. 1:4

2 Peter 3:13
^a Is. 65:17; 66:22
^b Rom. 8:21; Rev. 21:1
^c Is. 60:21; 65:25; Rev. 21:27

2 Peter 3:14
^a 1 Cor. 15:58; 2 Pet. 1:10
^b 2 Pet. 3:1
^c 1 Pet. 1:7
^d Phil. 2:15; 1 Thess. 5:23; 1 Tim. 6:14; James. 1:27

2 Peter 3:15
^a 2 Pet. 3:9

[b] Acts. 9:17; 15:25; 2 Pet. 3:2
[c] 1 Cor. 3:10; Eph. 3:3

2 Peter 3:16
[a] 2 Pet. 3:14
[b] Heb. 5:11
[c] 2 Pet. 2:14
[d] 2 Pet. 3:2

2 Peter 3:17
[a] 2 Pet. 3:1
[b] 1 Cor. 10:12
[c] 2 Pet. 2:18
[1] Or *disgraceful*
[d] 2 Pet. 2:7
[e] Rev. 2:5
[2] Or *firm hold*

2 Peter 3:18
[a] 2 Pet. 1:2
[b] 2 Pet. 1:11; 2:20
[c] Rom. 11:36; 2 Tim. 4:18; Rev. 1:6

Koine Greek

2Peter 3:1   Ταύτην ἤδη, ἀγαπητοί, δευτέραν ὑμῖν γράφω ἐπιστολήν ἐν αἷς διεγείρω ὑμῶν ἐν ὑπομνήσει τὴν εἰλικρινῆ διάνοιαν 2 μνησθῆναι τῶν προειρημένων ῥημάτων ὑπὸ τῶν ἁγίων προφητῶν καὶ τῆς τῶν ἀποστόλων ὑμῶν ἐντολῆς τοῦ κυρίου καὶ σωτῆρος. 3 τοῦτο πρῶτον γινώσκοντες ὅτι ἐλεύσονται ἐπ' ἐσχάτων τῶν ἡμερῶν ἐν ἐμπαιγμονῇ ἐμπαῖκται κατὰ τὰς ἰδίας ἐπιθυμίας αὐτῶν πορευόμενοι 4 καὶ λέγοντες· ποῦ ἐστιν ἡ ἐπαγγελία τῆς παρουσίας αὐτοῦ; ἀφ' ἧς γὰρ οἱ πατέρες ἐκοιμήθησαν, πάντα οὕτως διαμένει ἀπ' ἀρχῆς κτίσεως. 5 λανθάνει γὰρ αὐτοὺς τοῦτο θέλοντας ὅτι οὐρανοὶ ἦσαν ἔκπαλαι καὶ γῆ ἐξ ὕδατος καὶ δι' ὕδατος συνεστῶσα τῷ τοῦ θεοῦ λόγῳ 6 δι' ὃν ὁ τότε κόσμος ὕδατι κατακλυσθεὶς ἀπώλετο· 7 οἱ δὲ νῦν οὐρανοὶ καὶ ἡ γῆ τῷ αὐτῷ λόγῳ τεθησαυρισμένοι εἰσὶν πυρὶ τηρούμενοι εἰς ἡμέραν κρίσεως καὶ ἀπωλείας τῶν ἀσεβῶν ἀνθρώπων.

2Peter 3:8   Ἐν δὲ τοῦτο μὴ λανθανέτω ὑμᾶς, ἀγαπητοί, ὅτι μία ἡμέρα παρὰ κυρίῳ ὡς χίλια ἔτη καὶ χίλια ἔτη ὡς ἡμέρα μία. 9 οὐ βραδύνει κύριος τῆς ἐπαγγελίας, ὥς τινες βραδύτητα ἡγοῦνται, ἀλλὰ μακροθυμεῖ εἰς ὑμᾶς μὴ βουλόμενός τινας ἀπολέσθαι ἀλλὰ πάντας εἰς μετάνοιαν χωρῆσαι.

2Peter 3:10   Ἥξει δὲ ἡμέρα κυρίου ὡς κλέπτης ἐν ᾗ οἱ οὐρανοὶ ῥοιζηδὸν παρελεύσονται, στοιχεῖα δὲ καυσούμενα λυθήσεται, καὶ γῆ καὶ τὰ ἐν αὐτῇ ἔργα οὐχ εὑρεθήσεται. 11 Τούτων οὕτως πάντων λυομένων ποταποὺς δεῖ ὑπάρχειν ὑμᾶς ἐν ἁγίαις ἀναστροφαῖς καὶ εὐσεβείαις 12 προσδοκῶντας καὶ σπεύδοντας τὴν παρουσίαν τῆς τοῦ θεοῦ ἡμέρας δι' ἣν οὐρανοὶ πυρούμενοι λυθήσονται καὶ στοιχεῖα καυσούμενα τήκεται. 13 *καινοὺς* δὲ *οὐρανοὺς καὶ γῆν καινὴν* κατὰ τὸ ἐπάγγελμα αὐτοῦ προσδοκῶμεν ἐν οἷς δικαιοσύνη κατοικεῖ.

2Peter 3:14   Διό, ἀγαπητοί, ταῦτα προσδοκῶντες σπουδάσατε ἄσπιλοι καὶ ἀμώμητοι αὐτῷ εὑρεθῆναι ἐν εἰρήνῃ 15 καὶ τὴν τοῦ κυρίου ἡμῶν μακροθυμίαν σωτηρίαν ἡγεῖσθε, καθὼς καὶ ὁ ἀγαπητὸς ἡμῶν ἀδελφὸς Παῦλος κατὰ τὴν δοθεῖσαν αὐτῷ σοφίαν ἔγραψεν ὑμῖν, 16 ὡς καὶ ἐν πάσαις ταῖς ἐπιστολαῖς λαλῶν ἐν αὐταῖς περὶ τούτων ἐν αἷς ἐστιν δυσνόητά τινα ἃ οἱ ἀμαθεῖς καὶ ἀστήρικτοι στρεβλώσουσιν ὡς καὶ τὰς λοιπὰς γραφὰς πρὸς τὴν ἰδίαν αὐτῶν ἀπώλειαν.

2Peter 3:17   Ὑμεῖς οὖν, ἀγαπητοί, προγινώσκοντες φυλάσσεσθε, ἵνα μὴ τῇ τῶν ἀθέσμων πλάνῃ συναπαχθέντες ἐκπέσητε τοῦ ἰδίου στηριγμοῦ, 18 αυξάνετε δὲ ἐν χάριτι καὶ γνώσει τοῦ κυρίου ἡμῶν καὶ σωτῆρος Ἰησοῦ Χριστοῦ. αὐτῷ ἡ δόξα καὶ νῦν καὶ εἰς ἡμέραν αἰῶνος.

Language

Process of Discovery

Linguistics Section

Linguistic Structure

A 3:1   ᵃBeloved, this is now the second letter I am writing to you in which I am ᵇstirring up your sincere mind by way of a reminder, 2 to ᵃremember the words spoken beforehand by ᵇthe holy prophets and ᶜthe commandment of the Lord and Savior *spoken* by your apostles.

> **B** 3 ᵃKnow this first *of all,* that ᵇin the last days ᶜmockers will come with *their* mocking, ᵈfollowing after their own lusts, 4 and saying, "ᵃWhere is the promise of His ᵇcoming? For *ever* since the fathers ¹ᶜfell asleep, all things continue just as *they were* ᵈfrom the beginning of creation."

>> **C** 5 For ¹when they maintain this, it escapes their notice that ᵃby the word of God *the* heavens existed long ago and *the* earth was ᵇformed out of water and by water, 6 through which ᵃthe world at that time was ᵇdestroyed by being flooded with water. 7 But by His word ᵃthe present heavens and earth are being reserved for ᵇfire, kept for ᶜthe day of judgment and destruction of ungodly people.

>>> **D** 8   But do not let this one *fact* escape your notice, ᵃbeloved, that with the Lord one day is like a thousand years, and ᵇa thousand years like one day. 9 ᵃThe Lord is not slow about His promise, as some count slowness, but ᵇis patient toward you, ᶜnot willing for any to perish, but for all to come to repentance.

>> **C'** 10 But ᵃthe day of the Lord ᵇwill come like a thief, in which ᶜthe heavens ᵈwill pass away with a roar and the ᵉelements will be destroyed with intense heat, and ᶠthe earth and ¹its works will be ²discovered.

> **B'** 11   Since all these things are to be destroyed in this way, what sort of people ought you to be in holy conduct and godliness, 12 ᵃlooking for and hastening the coming of the day of God, because of which ᵇthe heavens will be destroyed by burning, and the ᶜelements will melt with intense heat! 13 But according to His ᵃpromise we are looking for ᵇnew heavens and a new earth, ᶜin which righteousness dwells.

A' 14 ᵃTherefore, ᵇbeloved, since you look for these things, be diligent to be ᶜfound ᵈspotless and blameless by Him, at peace, 15 and regard the ᵃpatience of our Lord *as* salvation; just as also ᵇour beloved brother Paul, ᶜaccording to the wisdom given him, wrote to you, 16 as also in all *his* letters, speaking in them of ᵃthese things, ᵇin which there are some things that are hard to understand, which the untaught and ᶜunstable distort, as *they do* also ᵈthe rest of the Scriptures, to their own destruction. 17 You therefore, ᵃbeloved, knowing this beforehand, ᵇbe on your guard so that you are not carried away by ᶜthe error of ¹ᵈunscrupulous people and ᵉlose your own ²firm commitment, 18 but grow in the grace and ᵃknowledge of our ᵇLord and Savior Jesus Christ. ᶜTo Him *be* the glory, both now and to the day of eternity. Amen.

Discussion

This chapter deals with the apocalypse, end times and final judgment.

Questioning the Passage

1. Who are the legates? (v. 2)

   Legates were Yeshua's apostles.

2. Who are the fathers in verse four?

   The term fathers in this verse is referring to the people's ancestors.

3. What does verse five and six mean?

   The author is addressing people who are denying the truth about God and His power. They are choosing to ignore the evidence of creation and the flood. "By the word of God, the heavens existed long ago and the earth was formed out of water and under water" refers to the creation account in Genesis, where God spoke the universe into existence. Peter emphasizes that the world was created by God's word, not by chance or natural processes.

The creation and the flood show God's absolute power over the universe. The author affirms the truthfulness of the Genesis account, even though some people deny it. Those who ignore God's word and His power will face judgment.

4. Why is fire in reserve for the day of judgment? (v. 7)
    The "fire at judgment day" is a metaphor used in the Bible to describe the ultimate consequences of sin and the separation from God. It is important to understand that this is not meant to be taken literally as a physical inferno. The Bible often uses fire as a symbol for God's purifying power, His wrath against sin, and the complete destruction of evil.

The "fire" represents the eternal separation from God that awaits those who reject His grace and forgiveness. This separation is described as a state of torment and anguish, often referred to as "hell" in Christian tradition. In some contexts, fire can also symbolize God's purifying power, refining and cleansing those who are faithful. This suggests that the "fire" is not only a punishment but also a means of ultimate justice and restoration.

Different Christian denominations and theological perspectives may interpret the "fire at judgment day" in slightly different ways. Some emphasize the literal aspect of fire, while others focus more on the symbolic meaning of separation from God.

Ultimately, the "fire at judgment day" serves as a powerful reminder of the seriousness of sin and the importance of seeking God's forgiveness and grace.

5. Why should people expect and desire the coming of the day of God? (v. 12)

This verse shows that the people were expecting the second coming of Yeshua when he would remove the oppressors. Messianic tradition says Messiah would do this on his "first visit." However, since Yeshua was called the Messiah, and it did not happen, Christian theology had to develop a reason. Their answer was that Yeshua will come a second time for the oppressors to be removed. The Zohar discusses the idea of having two messiahs. The first Messiah came to revive the spiritual awareness of the people, while the second one will take care of removing the oppressors from the land.

6. What is the patience of our Lord as salvation? (v. 15)

This verse is a call to discernment and vigilance for believers.

The author urged his readers to reflect carefully on what he has been teaching them about the return of Christ and the end times. They are warned against being deceived by false teachings and dangerous ideologies that contradict the truth of the Gospel. These "errors" could come from within the church or from outside sources.

A person could lose their salvation or spiritual standing. Peter emphasizes the importance of staying grounded in the truth and resisting any teachings that undermine the faith.

This verse comes at the end of this letter, where he has been addressing various issues facing the early church, including false teachers and the delay of Yeshua's return. He wants his readers to be prepared for these challenges and to remain steadfast in their faith.

By staying vigilant and grounded in the truth, we can avoid being misled and remain strong in our faith.

7. Was Paul's letters considered scripture when this letter was written? (v. 16) Scholars believe this letter was written around 150 CE. Paul's letters became sacred documents around 100 CE. Since this letter refers heavily to those Pauline letters, it supports the idea that their letter was written around 150 CE

Thoughts

That Yeshua was going to return and make things right is a strong part of the Christian tradition. It started in the beginning with Paul telling us that Yeshua will return in his lifetime. However, Yeshua has not returned. Therefore, the question of when is he going to return and why the delay became prominent in the Christian community and still is today.

Bibliography

"1 Peter 1:11." BibleRef.com. Accessed July 5, 2024. https://www.bibleref.com/1-Peter/1/1-Peter-1-11.html.

"1 Peter 1:5 - Verse-by-Verse Bible Commentary." StudyLight.org. Accessed July 5, 2024. https://www.studylight.org/commentary/1-peter/1-5.html.

"1 Peter 2:12." BibleRef.com. Accessed July 17, 2024. https://www.bibleref.com/1-Peter/2/1-Peter-2-12.html.

"1 Peter 3:1." BibleRef.com. Accessed July 31, 2024. https://www.bibleref.com/1-Peter/3/1-Peter-3-1.html.

Aramaic light on james through revelation: Rocco A. Errico and George M. Lamsa: 9780976008026: Amazon.com: Books. Accessed July 5, 2024. https://www.amazon.com/Aramaic-Light-James-through-Revelation/dp/0976008025.

Gerencser, Bruce. "Christian Patriarchy: Should Wives Obey Their Husbands No Matter What?" The Life and Times of Bruce Gerencser, December 2, 2021. https://brucegerencser.net/2019/03/christian-patriarchy-should-wives-obey-their-husbands-no-matter-what/.

The meaning of 1 peter 3:17 explained. Accessed July 31, 2024. https://www.scripturespeaks.org/verse/1+peter+3%3A17.

Says, The Bible. "1 Peter 1:20-21 Meaning." TheBibleSays.com, June 13, 2024. https://thebiblesays.com/en/commentary/1pe+1:20?slug=null.

user35953user35953, LucianLucian 17911 gold badge88 silver badges2424 bronze badges, DottardDottard 110k55 gold badges4949 silver badges161161 bronze badges, agarzaagarza 14k55 gold badges4343 silver badges8888 bronze badges, Ozzie OzzieOzzie Ozzie 4, and bronze badges. "What's Wrong with Braided Hair in 1 Timothy 2:9?" Biblical Hermeneutics Stack Exchange, February 1, 1966. https://hermeneutics.stackexchange.com/questions/50086/whats-wrong-with-braided-hair-in-1-timothy-29.

www.ingramcontent.com/pod-product-compliance
Lightning Source LLC
Chambersburg PA
CBHW081217130726
47997CB00009B/2681